The Best of Mr. Food®

Fix It Fast!

"With this all-new collection of recipes, you're guaranteed to get in and out of the kitchen—fast!"

Giant Ham-and-Pepper Salad Sandwich,
page 155

Chipotle-Cinnamon Pork Chop,
page 135

Banana-Berry Split,
page 198

The Best of Mr. Food®

Fix It Fast!

Oxmoor House®

ISBN-13: 978-0-8487-3225-7
ISBN-10: 0-8487-3225-1
Library of Congress Control Number: 2007941809

Printed in the United States of America
First Printing 2008

Mr. Food® and OOH IT'S SO GOOD!!® are registered marks owned by
Ginsburg Enterprises Incorporated.

Ginsburg Enterprises Incorporated
    Chief Executive Officer: Art Ginsburg
    Chief Operating Officer: Steve Ginsburg
    Vice President, Publishing: Caryl Ginsburg Fantel
    Vice President, Creative Business Development: Howard Rosenthal

Oxmoor House, Inc.
    Editor in Chief: Nancy Fitzpatrick Wyatt
    Executive Editor: Susan Carlisle Payne
    Art Director: Keith McPherson
    Managing Editor: Allison Long Lowery

THE BEST OF MR. FOOD® FIX IT FAST!, featuring the recipes of
Mr. Food, Art Ginsburg
    Editor: Kelly Hooper Troiano
    Project Editor: Terri Laschober Robertson
    Senior Designer: Melissa Jones Clark
    Copy Chief: L. Amanda Owens
    Editorial Assistant: Amelia Heying
    Director, Test Kitchens: Elizabeth Tyler Austin
    Assistant Director, Test Kitchens: Julie Christopher
    Test Kitchens Professionals: Jane Chambliss; Patricia Michaud; Kathleen Royal
    Phillips; Catherine Crowell Steele; Ashley T. Strickland; Kate Wheeler, R.D.
    Photography Director: Jim Bathie
    Senior Photo Stylist: Kay E. Clarke
    Associate Photo Stylist: Katherine Eckert
    Director of Production: Laura Lockhart
    Production Manager: Tamara B. Nall

Contributors
    Designer: Carol Damsky
    Copy Editor: Francesca Baldone Allen
    Indexer: Mary Ann Laurens
    Proofreader: Barzella Papa
    Interns: Tracey Apperson, Carol Corbin, Erin Loudy

Cover: Skillet Ziti (page 13)

Contents

Welcome!!

"Fix It Fast! is your busy family's solution for home-cooked meals on the table in 30 minutes or less—no kidding! You'll discover simple recipes using ingredients that you probably already have on hand. As you've come to expect in my books, you'll always find enticing entrées, savory sides and salads, and scrumptious soups and sandwiches. Also included are:

- 10 one-dish meals you can make using ingredients you probably already have in your pantry. We supply the list to get you started.
- Savory recipes that make one meal…and then I tell you how to transform leftovers into another new and exciting meal for the next night. You'll never look at leftovers the same way again—I call 'em 'planned-overs'!
- Recipes for the health-conscious—complete with nutritional analyses
- Snacks for all ages and occasions, as well as dazzling desserts to complete any meal

From start to finish, you'll be out of the kitchen fast. Here's how we help:

- A banner runs at the top of each recipe to give you a heads-up for finding just the right recipe. Whether you're looking for something fast, with few ingredients, suitable for a special occasion, or especially for the kids, it's here at a glance!
- Prep and cook times keep you on track with each recipe.
- Recipe tips give you insight on ingredients and cooking techniques.
- Easy-to-find ingredients and numbered step-by-step instructions make cooking a breeze!

With over 170 recipes to choose from, the meal planning is done, and 'OOH IT'S SO GOOD!!®' Enjoy!**"**

Mr. Food

Pantry Suppers

"By stocking your kitchen with ingredients from the grocery list on the following page, you can always have one of these 10 ingenious recipes ready in a jiffy. Cook one up tonight!**"**

25 Ingredients = 10 Meals

Keep these 25 items on hand; with them and a few basic staples, you'll be able to whip up 10 one-dish-meal recipes in 30 minutes or less!

In the freezer:
1. ground round
2. boneless pork loin chops
3. pork tenderloin
4. chicken breasts (skinned and boned), chopped cooked chicken
5. white fish fillets, tuna steaks
6. frozen peeled raw shrimp
7. frozen chopped onions, frozen seasoning blend
8. frozen mixed vegetables

In the refrigerator:
9. vegetables: bagged baby spinach, sliced carrots
10. cheeses: preshredded Parmesan, sharp Cheddar, Italian six-cheese blend
11. sour cream
12. bacon
13. smoked sausage
14. flour tortillas

In the pantry:
15. biscuit baking mix
16. pasta: elbow macaroni, ziti
17. boil-in-bag white rice: extra-large bags, regular-size bags
18. canned beans: cannellini, black
19. canned diced tomatoes: plain; flavored with basil, garlic, and oregano; and with green chilies
20. chicken broth
21. cream soup: chicken, mushroom, celery
22. barbecue sauce
23. pasta sauce: tomato and basil
24. salsa, chunky
25. olives: kalamata, Spanish

Staples

Keep these basic items, from the fridge and pantry, always on hand. They're versatile enough to use in a wide variety of recipes.

- fat-free balsamic vinaigrette
- cornstarch
- eggs
- all-purpose flour
- prepared minced garlic
- lemon juice
- milk
- oil: canola, olive
- salt
- black pepper: ground, peppercorns
- soy sauce
- Worcestershire sauce

Herbs & Seasoning Blends:
- Cajun seasoning
- chili powder
- cumin, ground
- oregano
- red pepper, crushed

Tex-Mex Lasagna

8 servings

prep: 7 minutes   cook: 23 minutes

1½ pounds ground round
1   teaspoon prepared minced garlic

1   (15-ounce) can black beans, drained
       and rinsed
1   (8-ounce) package preshredded
       sharp Cheddar cheese, divided
2   tablespoons chili powder
½   teaspoon ground cumin
1   (10-ounce) can diced tomatoes with
       green chilies, drained
1   (8-ounce) container sour cream
1   (16-ounce) bottled chunky salsa
6   (10") flour tortillas

1 Preheat the oven to 425°. Cook beef and garlic in a large nonstick skillet over medium-high heat, stirring until the beef crumbles and is no longer pink; drain.

2 Combine beef mixture, black beans, 1 cup cheese, and the next 5 ingredients. Line a lightly greased 9" x 13" baking dish with 2 tortillas. Spoon ⅓ of beef mixture over tortillas. Repeat layers twice. Sprinkle with remaining cheese.

3 Bake at 425° for 15 minutes or until cheese melts.

" *¡Hola, amigos! Check out my Tex-Mex take on a classic Italian dish. This lasagna is layered with yummy tortillas and black beans and then spiced up with green chilies and chunky salsa.* **"**

Veggie Beef Casserole

8 servings

prep: 6 minutes   cook: 24 minutes

8   ounces uncooked elbow macaroni

1¼   pounds ground round
1   tablespoon canola oil
1   (16-ounce) bag frozen mixed
        vegetables, thawed
1   (10¾-ounce) can cream of
        mushroom soup, undiluted
1   cup milk
½   teaspoon dried oregano
¼   teaspoon ground black pepper
1   teaspoon Worcestershire sauce

1   (10¾-ounce) can cream of celery
        soup, undiluted
½   cup (2 ounces) shredded sharp
        Cheddar cheese

1 Cook pasta according to package directions. Drain and set aside.

2 Meanwhile, preheat the oven to 425°. Cook beef in a large skillet over medium-high heat, stirring until it crumbles and is no longer pink; drain and set beef aside. Heat oil in same skillet over medium heat; add vegetables, and sauté 2 minutes. Stir in cream of mushroom soup and next 4 ingredients. Bring to a boil, stirring constantly. Reduce heat to medium, and cook 4 minutes or until thickened.

3 Combine pasta, beef, vegetable mixture, and celery soup in a large bowl. Spoon mixture into a lightly greased 9" x 13" baking dish. Sprinkle with cheese.

4 Bake, uncovered, at 425° for 10 minutes or until cheese is melted.

"Lookin' for a dish that'll be a sure crowd-pleaser? Then look no further! Loaded with veggies and beef and topped with cheese, this casserole mixes up in a snap and will vanish just as quickly!"

Skillet Ziti

(pictured on cover)

8 servings

prep: 4 minutes   cook: 26 minutes

8	ounces uncooked ziti
1	pound ground round
1	(10-ounce) package frozen chopped onions, thawed and drained well
½	teaspoon salt
¼	teaspoon freshly ground black pepper
1	(26-ounce) jar tomato and basil pasta sauce
1	(8-ounce) container sour cream
⅓	cup shredded Parmesan cheese
1	(8-ounce) package shredded Italian six-cheese blend

1 Cook pasta according to package directions. Drain and set aside.

2 While pasta cooks, cook beef, onions, salt, and pepper in a large skillet over medium-high heat, stirring until the beef crumbles and is no longer pink; drain.

3 Stir in pasta sauce; cook 1 minute or until thoroughly heated. Add pasta, stirring to coat.

4 Combine sour cream and Parmesan cheese. Stir into pasta mixture. Sprinkle Italian cheese blend over pasta mixture. Cover, reduce heat to medium, and cook 5 minutes or until cheese melts.

"My ziti-in-a-skillet cooks up twice as fast as the traditional oven-baked version—plus it's creamier and cheesier!"

Pork Medallions over Wilted Spinach

4 servings

prep: 12 minutes   cook: 12 minutes

4   slices bacon

1   (1¼- to 1½-pound) pork tenderloin
¼   teaspoon salt
½   teaspoon pepper
¼   cup all-purpose flour

½   cup fat-free balsamic vinaigrette
½   cup chicken broth
½   cup frozen chopped onion

1   (6-ounce) bag baby spinach

Make It Fast!

For speedy prep work, place all 8 pork slices between 2 large sheets of plastic wrap and flatten quickly with a few whacks of the rolling pin!

1 Cook bacon in a large skillet over medium-high heat until crisp; remove bacon, and drain on paper towels, reserving drippings in skillet. Crumble bacon, and set aside.

2 While bacon cooks, cut tenderloin crosswise into 8 slices (medallions). Place slices between 2 sheets of heavy-duty plastic wrap; flatten to ¼" thickness, using a meat mallet or rolling pin. Sprinkle pork with salt and pepper. Place flour in a shallow dish; dredge pork in flour, shaking off excess flour.

3 Heat bacon drippings in skillet over medium-high heat. Add pork, and cook 2 to 3 minutes on each side or until done. Remove pork from pan, and keep warm.

4 Combine balsamic vinaigrette, chicken broth, and onion; add to pan. Cook 3 minutes or until mixture is reduced by about one-half. Add pork to pan; cook 1 to 2 minutes or until pork slices are warmed and coated with sauce. Remove pork from pan.

5 Place spinach in a large bowl; pour warm vinaigrette mixture over spinach. Sprinkle with crumbled bacon, and toss well until spinach is lightly wilted. Divide spinach mixture evenly among serving plates; top with pork medallions.

Smothered Pork Chops over Rice

4 servings

prep: 5 minutes   cook: 13 minutes

2	extra-large bags boil-in-bag white rice
2	tablespoons all-purpose flour
2	teaspoons chili powder, divided
1	teaspoon salt
⅛	teaspoon pepper
4	(½"-thick) boneless pork loin chops
2	tablespoons canola oil
½	cup bottled barbecue sauce
¼	cup frozen chopped onion
¼	cup water
2	teaspoons cornstarch
2	teaspoons water

1 Prepare rice according to package directions; keep warm.

2 Meanwhile, combine flour, 1 teaspoon chili powder, the salt, and pepper in a shallow dish; dredge pork chops in flour mixture.

3 Heat oil in a large nonstick skillet over medium-high heat. Add chops, and cook 2 minutes on each side or until golden.

4 Combine barbecue sauce, onion, ¼ cup water, and remaining 1 teaspoon chili powder; pour over chops. Cover, reduce heat, and simmer 8 minutes or until chops are done. Remove chops from pan, and keep warm.

5 Combine cornstarch and 2 teaspoons water, stirring until smooth. Add cornstarch mixture to sauce in pan; cook, stirring constantly, 1 minute. Divide rice evenly among plates; place chops over rice, and spoon sauce evenly over chops.

Slurry in a Hurry

Adding a slurry is a fast and easy way to thicken a sauce with no lumping. A mixture of cornstarch (or flour) and water is stirred into a hot liquid mixture, as we do in this recipe.

Chicken and Sausage Jambalaya

6 servings

prep: 6 minutes   cook: 21 minutes

1   pound skinned and boned chicken
      breasts, cut into 1 pieces
2   teaspoons Cajun seasoning, divided

2   teaspoons canola oil
1   pound smoked sausage, sliced

1   (10-ounce) package frozen seasoning
      blend, thawed and drained
2   teaspoons prepared minced garlic
1   (14½-ounce) can diced tomatoes
      with zesty mild green chilies,
      undrained
1   extra-large bag boil-in-bag white rice,
      removed from bag
1½ cups chicken broth

1 Combine chicken and 1 teaspoon Cajun seasoning in a bowl.

2 Heat oil in a Dutch oven over medium-high heat. Add sausage and chicken; sauté 6 minutes or until browned on all sides. Remove from pan; drain.

3 Add seasoning blend and garlic to pan; sauté 2 minutes or until heated thoroughly. Add sausage, chicken, remaining 1 teaspoon Cajun seasoning, the tomatoes, rice, and broth to pan. Bring to a boil; cover and boil 11 minutes or until liquid is absorbed, stirring halfway through cooking time.

"I call for boil-in-bag rice to speed up the cooking time of this Creole favorite. But instead of cooking the rice separately in its bag, we add it straight to the pan so it can absorb the liquid and all the savory flavors as it cooks.**"**

Creamy Chicken 'n' Dumplings

6 servings

prep: 11 minutes   cook: 19 minutes

1   tablespoon canola oil
½   cup frozen chopped onions
1½ cups thinly sliced carrots

2   (10¾-ounce) cans cream of chicken
       soup
3½ cups water
4   cups chopped cooked chicken

2   cups biscuit baking mix
¾   cup milk
Freshly ground black pepper

1 Heat oil in a Dutch oven over medium heat. Add onions and carrots; cover and cook 5 minutes or until tender, stirring often.

2 Stir soup, water, and chicken into vegetable mixture. Bring mixture to a boil.

3 Meanwhile, combine baking mix and milk in a medium bowl. Reduce heat to simmer; drop dough in 12 mounds onto simmering chicken mixture. Cover and simmer 10 minutes or until a toothpick inserted in center of dumplings comes out clean. Ladle mixture evenly into pasta or soup bowls; sprinkle with pepper. Serve immediately.

"*No need to simmer this pot of chicken 'n' dumplings all day. Use a rotisserie chicken to save time as well as for convenience. For 4 cups of chopped cooked chicken, you'll need 1½ to 2 chickens. And biscuit baking mix provides an easy shortcut to hand-rolled dumplings. This is a dish that would have made Mama proud!***"**

Mediterranean Fish Fillets over Rice

4 servings

prep: 5 minutes   cook: 18 minutes

4   (6-ounce) frozen firm white fish
     fillets, thawed (*see tip*)
¾   teaspoon salt
½   teaspoon pepper
1½   tablespoons olive oil

1   (14½-ounce) can diced tomatoes
     with basil, garlic, and oregano,
     undrained
½   cup pitted kalamata olives, halved
2   tablespoons lemon juice
1   teaspoon prepared minced garlic
Warm cooked rice

1 Pat fish fillets dry with paper towels;
sprinkle with salt and pepper. Heat oil
in a large nonstick skillet over medium-
high heat. Add fish; cook 3 to 4 minutes
on each side or until browned.

2 Add tomatoes and next 3 ingredients
to skillet. Cover, reduce heat, and
simmer 9 to 10 minutes or until fish
flakes easily with a fork. Serve fish and
tomato mixture over warm rice.

Savory Substitutes

Any firm white fish fillets, such as orange roughy, grouper,
or red snapper, will work well in this Mediterranean-inspired
dish. And if you have feta or Parmesan cheese on hand,
sprinkle it over the fish before serving.

Seared Tuna with White Bean Salad

4 servings

prep: 10 minutes   cook: 7 minutes

⅔ cup fat-free balsamic vinaigrette
2   tablespoons lemon juice

4   (6-ounce) frozen tuna steaks, thawed
2   tablespoons olive oil
Salt and pepper to taste

1   (15½-ounce) can cannellini beans,
       drained and rinsed
1   (14½-ounce) can diced tomatoes,
       drained
½ cup Spanish olives, chopped
1   (6-ounce) package baby spinach

1 Whisk together vinaigrette and lemon juice in a small bowl. Set dressing aside.

2 Brush tuna with oil; sprinkle with salt and pepper. Heat a large nonstick skillet over medium-high heat. Add tuna, and cook 3 minutes on each side or until fish flakes easily with a fork. Remove from pan, and keep warm.

3 Combine beans, tomatoes, and olives in a medium bowl; toss with ¼ cup of dressing. Place spinach in a large bowl; toss with 2 tablespoons dressing.

4 Divide spinach evenly among 4 plates; top evenly with white bean salad. Top each serving with tuna; drizzle with remaining dressing.

"Don't let the canned products fool you. With fresh spinach and tangy lemon, this dish is full of fresh taste and ooh-so-goodness!**"**

Shrimp Fried Rice

(pictured on page 106)

4 servings

prep: 2 minutes   cook: 21 minutes

2   (3.5-ounce) bags quick-cooking long-
     grain rice (see tip)

3   tablespoons canola oil, divided
2   large eggs, lightly beaten

1   teaspoon prepared minced garlic
¼   teaspoon crushed red pepper
1   pound peeled and deveined frozen
     raw shrimp, thawed
1½   cups frozen mixed vegetables,
     thawed
3   tablespoons soy sauce

1 Cook rice according to package directions; set aside.

2 Meanwhile, place 1 tablespoon oil in a large skillet over medium-high heat. Add eggs; cook 1 to 2 minutes, stirring frequently until scrambled. Remove from skillet, and set aside.

3 Heat remaining 2 tablespoons oil in skillet; add garlic, crushed red pepper, and shrimp. Cook 2 minutes or until shrimp turn pink. Add vegetables, and cook until thoroughly heated. Stir in soy sauce, reserved rice, and scrambled eggs; cook 1 minute or until thoroughly heated.

Twice as Nice
Use leftover rice, or make rice ahead and refrigerate, to help get supper on the table in a hurry. Starting with cooked and chilled rice not only saves time, but the end product is better.

Double-Duty Meals

"Two different meals from one recipe? You betcha! 'Planned-overs' from 12 main-dish recipes are morphed into 13 new meals. You'll never look at leftovers the same way again!"

Southwest Sausage Chili

12½ cups (save 6¼ cups for Cornbread-Topped Sausage Chili Bake)

prep: 4 minutes   cook: 26 minutes

2	pounds ground Italian sausage
½	cup minced onion
2	(16-ounce) cans kidney beans, rinsed and drained
2	(7-ounce) cans whole kernel corn with sweet red pepper
2	(15-ounce) cans tomato sauce
1⅓	cups salsa
1⅓	cups water
2	teaspoons chili powder
½	teaspoon freshly ground black pepper
½	teaspoon ground cumin
¼	teaspoon salt

1 Cook sausage and onion in a Dutch oven over medium-high heat, stirring until the sausage crumbles and is no longer pink; drain.

2 Stir in beans and remaining 8 ingredients. Bring to a boil over medium-high heat. Reduce heat to medium; simmer, uncovered, for 12 minutes or until thoroughly heated, stirring often.

3 Reserve half of chili for Cornbread-Topped Sausage Chili Bake, if desired. Serve remaining chili with chopped scallions and sour cream, if desired.

"*This dish is a real crowd-pleaser! They'll think you've been home cookin' all day—but we'll keep that secret to ourselves.***"**

Cornbread-Topped Sausage Chili Bake

8 servings

prep: 6 minutes   cook: 20 minutes

1   (8½-ounce) package corn muffin mix
1   large egg, lightly beaten
⅓   cup milk

½   Southwest Sausage Chili recipe
      (about 6¼ cups) (opposite page)
Sour cream

1 Preheat the oven to 400°. Whisk together first 3 ingredients in a medium bowl.

2 Spoon chili into a lightly greased 9" x 13" baking dish. Spoon batter over chili. Bake, uncovered, at 400° for 20 minutes or until cornbread is lightly browned. Serve with sour cream.

"*Instead of serving your chili with a side of cornbread, how 'bout serving the cornbread atop your chili?! Wow!***"**

Dutch Oven-Roasted Greek Chicken

4 servings (plus 4 chicken breasts and half of tomato mixture for
Greek Chicken Pita Pockets)

prep: 5 minutes   cook: 25 minutes

2	tablespoons olive oil
8	(6-ounce) boneless skinless chicken breasts
2	teaspoons Greek seasoning
2	cups cherry tomatoes
1	large onion, vertically halved and thinly sliced
½	cup pitted kalamata olives, halved
3	cloves garlic, minced
1	tablespoon lemon juice

1 Heat oil in a 6-quart Dutch oven over medium-high heat. Sprinkle chicken breasts evenly with Greek seasoning. Brown chicken in batches 3 minutes on each side. Remove chicken from pan, and keep warm.

2 Add tomatoes, onion, and olives to pan; cover and cook over medium-high heat 5 minutes or until tomatoes begin to burst, stirring frequently. Stir in garlic and chicken. Cover and cook over medium-high heat 8 minutes or until chicken is done and onion is tender. Remove chicken from pan. Stir lemon juice into tomato mixture in pan.

3 Divide tomato mixture in half. Reserve 4 chicken breasts and half of tomato mixture for Greek Chicken Pita Pockets, if desired. Place remaining 4 chicken breasts on a serving platter. Spoon remaining half of tomato mixture over chicken.

"*These savory chicken breasts are 'roasted' in a Dutch oven on the stovetop for quick and easy convenience.***"**

Greek Chicken Pita Pockets

4 servings

prep: 26 minutes   cook: 2 minutes

1	cup finely chopped English cucumber (see tip)
¼	teaspoon salt
1	(8-ounce) container plain fat-free yogurt
1	teaspoon chopped fresh mint or ⅓ teaspoon dried mint
½	teaspoon lemon juice
½	teaspoon prepared minced garlic
4	Dutch Oven-Roasted Greek Chicken breasts, sliced (opposite page)
½	tomato mixture (from Dutch Oven-Roasted Greek Chicken, opposite page)
4	green leaf lettuce leaves, halved lengthwise
4	(7") pita bread rounds, halved and split
½	cup crumbled feta cheese

1 Combine first 6 ingredients in a small bowl; cover and chill until ready to serve.

2 Combine sliced chicken and tomato mixture in a medium-sized microwave-safe bowl. Microwave at HIGH 2 minutes or just until warm.

3 Place a lettuce leaf half in each pita half. Top with warmed chicken mixture, cucumber sauce, and cheese. Serve immediately.

Know Your "Cukes"

English cucumbers are seedless, and they're longer and thinner than regular cucumbers. There's no need to peel them—just be sure to wash thoroughly to remove the waxy finish, which helps to prolong the freshness of supermarket cucumbers.

Grilled 'Bello Burgers

4 servings (plus 4 grilled mushrooms for Creamy Mushroom Risotto)

prep: 4 minutes   cook: 10 minutes

Nonstick cooking spray
8   (4") portobello mushrooms (see tip)
4   (¼") slices red onion
⅓   cup balsamic vinaigrette

¼   cup mayonnaise
2   tablespoons chopped fresh basil
      (see note)

4   kaiser sandwich rolls
4   slices provolone cheese
4   (¼") slices tomato
4   green leaf lettuce leaves

1 Spray cold grill rack with nonstick cooking spray. Preheat the grill to medium-high heat (350° to 400°). Place mushrooms and onion slices on grill rack; brush half of vinaigrette over mushrooms. Grill vegetables, covered, 5 minutes on each side or until tender, brushing mushrooms with remaining vinaigrette when turned.

2 Reserve 4 grilled mushrooms for Creamy Mushroom Risotto, if desired.

3 Meanwhile, combine mayonnaise and basil; set aside.

4 To serve, place 1 mushroom on bottom half of each roll. Top with provolone cheese, grilled onion slices, tomato slices, and lettuce leaves. Spread mayonnaise mixture evenly on each remaining roll half; place top of bun on lettuce. Serve immediately.

Note: To chop fresh basil, tightly roll leaves, and cut with a knife or kitchen shears.

Where's the Beef?

You won't miss any beef in these hearty portobello burgers! These mushrooms have huge caps that have a meaty flavor and texture.

Creamy Mushroom Risotto

4 servings

prep: 3 minutes   cook: 27 minutes

3   cups chicken broth

1   tablespoon butter
½   cup finely chopped onion
1   teaspoon prepared minced garlic
1   cup uncooked Arborio rice

4   grilled portobello mushrooms,
      coarsely chopped (opposite page)
¼   teaspoon freshly ground black
      pepper
¼   teaspoon dried thyme
¼   cup grated Parmesan cheese

1 Bring chicken broth to a simmer in a medium saucepan (do not boil). Keep warm over low heat.

2 Meanwhile, melt butter in a large saucepan over medium heat. Add onion, garlic, and rice; cook, stirring constantly, 4 minutes or until onion is tender. Add ½ cup hot broth, stirring constantly, until liquid is nearly absorbed. Repeat procedure, adding remaining broth, ½ cup at a time, stirring constantly until each portion of broth is absorbed before adding next portion (about 22 minutes total).

3 Remove from heat; stir in mushrooms and remaining ingredients. Serve immediately.

Take It Easy!

Don't be tempted to speed up the cooking process. The goal is to get a creamy rice dish, with the center of the rice left with just a little bit of crunch to it. In a half hour, dinner will be served!

Ragu alla Bolognese

4 servings (plus 4 cups sauce for Florentine Lasagna Rolls)

prep: 16 minutes   cook: 8½ hours

1   pound lean ground beef (see tip)
1   pound ground pork (see tip)
1   (8-ounce) container chopped onion, celery, and green bell pepper (see note)
2   medium carrots, finely chopped
1   teaspoon prepared minced garlic

2   (14½-ounce) cans diced tomatoes in sauce
½   cup dry red wine or beef broth
2   teaspoons dried basil
1   teaspoon salt
¼   teaspoon freshly ground black pepper
1   cup milk

8   ounces uncooked fettuccine

1 Cook first 5 ingredients in a large skillet over medium-high heat 8 minutes or until the meat crumbles and is no longer pink; drain and place in a 3½- to 4-quart slow cooker.

2 Stir tomatoes and next 4 ingredients into meat mixture. Cover and cook on LOW setting 8 hours. Stir in milk; cover and cook 30 more minutes.

3 Cook pasta according to package directions; drain. Reserve 4 cups sauce for Florentine Lasagna Rolls, if desired. Serve remaining 4 cups sauce over pasta.

Note: You can find pre-chopped onion, celery, and green bell pepper in a container in the produce section of your supermarket.

That's Italian!

Bolognese is a thick Italian pasta sauce that's made from ground meat, tomatoes, celery, and carrots and seasoned with garlic and herbs. Some supermarkets have a pre-mixed meat loaf mixture available. Feel free to use that in place of the ground beef and pork—just be sure the meat loaf mixture doesn't contain bread crumbs.

Florentine Lasagna Rolls

4 to 8 servings

prep: 5 minutes   cook: 25 minutes

1   (10-ounce) package frozen chopped
        spinach, thawed and drained
1   (16-ounce) container ricotta cheese
½   cup grated Parmesan cheese
¼   teaspoon freshly ground black
        pepper
8   lasagna noodles, cooked

4   cups warm Ragu alla Bolognese
        (opposite page)
1½ cups (6 ounces) shredded mozzarella
        cheese

1 Stir together first 4 ingredients in a medium bowl. Spread mixture evenly over lasagna noodles; roll up, and place seam sides down in a lightly greased 8" x 12" baking dish.

2 Pour Ragu alla Bolognese over lasagna rolls, and sprinkle with mozzarella cheese. Microwave, uncovered, at HIGH 8 minutes or until thoroughly heated.

Serve It Up!

This recipe makes 8 lasagna rolls with a meaty sauce. For heartier appetites, plan on 4 servings. If you're serving extra sides, it will probably be good for 8 servings.

Marinated Grilled Chicken Thighs

4 servings (plus 4 thighs for Easy Chicken Chimis)

prep: 5 minutes   cook: 12 minutes   marinate: 10 minutes

2   tablespoons brown sugar
2   tablespoons Worcestershire sauce
2   tablespoons soy sauce
1   tablespoon sesame seeds
1   tablespoon prepared minced garlic
1   tablespoon sesame oil
1   tablespoon molasses
1   teaspoon paprika
¾   teaspoon garlic salt
¼   teaspoon pepper
¼   cup canola oil
12   skinless, boneless chicken thighs

1 Combine first 11 ingredients in a large resealable plastic freezer bag; add chicken. Seal and marinate in the refrigerator while grill is preheating. Meanwhile, preheat the grill to medium-high heat (350° to 400°).

2 Remove chicken from bag, reserving marinade. Place reserved marinade in a saucepan, and bring to a boil; boil 1 minute. Grill chicken, covered, 4 to 5 minutes on each side or until done, basting with reserved boiled marinade.

3 Serve 2 thighs per serving for dinner, and reserve 4 thighs for Easy Chicken Chimis, if desired.

❝Don't let this short marinating time fool you—these juicy chicken thighs are loaded with savory flavor.**❞**

Easy Chicken Chimis

4 servings

prep: 7 minutes   cook: 13 minutes

1   (10.5-ounce) can cream of chicken
     soup, undiluted
1   (4.5-ounce) can diced green chilies
2   tablespoons pimiento-stuffed
     Spanish olives (about 12)
2   tablespoons pickled jalapeño
     peppers
2   tablespoons lime juice

1   (8-ounce) package cream cheese,
     softened
1   (8-ounce) package shredded
     Monterey Jack cheese
½   (1¼-ounce) package reduced-sodium
     taco seasoning
4   Marinated Grilled Chicken Thighs,
     chopped (opposite page)
4   (10") flour tortillas

3   tablespoons vegetable oil

1 Process first 5 ingredients in a food
processor until smooth, stopping to
scrape down sides as needed. Pour soup
mixture into a medium saucepan; cook
over medium-low heat 5 minutes or until
thoroughly heated, stirring occasionally.
Remove sauce from heat, and keep warm.

2 Stir together cream cheese and next 3
ingredients. Spoon cream cheese mixture evenly down the center of each tortilla.
Fold sides in, and roll up burrito-style.

3 Heat oil in a large skillet over medium-
high heat. Place chimichangas seam-
side down in skillet. Fry 2 minutes on each
side or until golden.

4 Top with sauce, and, if desired, serve
with chopped scallions, shredded
Cheddar cheese, and sour cream.

" *These chimichangas are pan-fried
favorites that are packed full of Mexican
flavor and flair. ¡Olé!* **"**

Beefed-Up Kabobs

8 kabobs (save 4 kabobs for Beef Stroganoff)

prep: 15 minutes   cook: 12 minutes   marinate: 8 hours

2   cups beef broth
1   cup olive oil
½   cup Worcestershire sauce
4   cloves garlic, minced
1   (3-pound) sirloin roast, cut into
        1" cubes
2   (8-ounce) packages fresh whole
        button mushrooms
1   large onion, cut into wedges

Nonstick cooking spray
½   teaspoon salt
½   teaspoon pepper

1 Combine beef broth and next 3 ingredients in a shallow dish or large resealable plastic freezer bag; add beef, mushrooms, and onion. Cover or seal, and chill 8 hours.

2 Coat cold grill rack with nonstick cooking spray. Preheat the grill to medium-high heat (350° to 400°). Remove steak and vegetables from marinade, discarding marinade. Thread steak and vegetables onto 8 (12") skewers (see tip). Sprinkle kabobs evenly with salt and pepper.

3 Grill, covered, 10 to 12 minutes or until desired degree of doneness, turning after 5 minutes. Reserve 4 kabobs for Beef Stroganoff, if desired.

The Edge on Skewers

If you use wooden skewers, be sure to soak them in water 30 minutes before threading and grilling the meat and veggies—if not, they'll burn as the food cooks. And no matter what type of skewers you use, always leave some space between the chunks of food when threading the kabobs so that the food will cook evenly.

Beef Stroganoff

4 servings

prep: 5 minutes   cook: 25 minutes

8	ounces uncooked egg noodles
2	tablespoons vegetable oil, divided
4	grilled Beefed-Up Kabobs, coarsely chopped (opposite page)
1	tablespoon all-purpose flour
2	cups beef broth
1	tablespoon Dijon mustard
1	(8-ounce) container sour cream
2	teaspoons lemon juice
1	tablespoon chopped fresh parsley or 1 teaspoon dried parsley

1 Cook noodles according to package directions; drain and keep warm.

2 Meanwhile, heat 1 tablespoon oil in a large skillet over medium-high heat. Add chopped meat and vegetables from kabobs, and cook 3 to 4 minutes or until thoroughly heated. Remove from skillet, and set aside.

3 Add remaining 1 tablespoon oil to skillet, and heat until hot. Gradually whisk in flour, and cook, whisking constantly, 3 minutes or until flour mixture smells "nutty." Whisk in beef broth; bring mixture to a boil, stirring constantly. Remove from heat; stir in mustard, sour cream, and lemon juice. Return beef and vegetables to skillet, and reheat, if necessary, over medium heat (do not boil). Stir in parsley, and serve over egg noodles.

❝*This hearty Russian specialty is sure to please the whole family. It's traditionally served over egg noodles, but hot cooked rice is great, too, to soak up the creamy sauce.* **❞**

Herbed Dijon Chicken

4 servings (save 4 chicken cutlets for Dijon Chicken Pizza)

prep: 5 minutes   cook: 22 minutes

12 (3-ounce) chicken cutlets
½   teaspoon salt
¼   teaspoon pepper

2   tablespoons olive oil

½   cup honey
½   cup Dijon mustard
1   teaspoon dried basil
1   teaspoon paprika
½   teaspoon dried parsley
½   teaspoon dried oregano

1 Sprinkle chicken cutlets with salt and pepper.

2 Heat olive oil in a large nonstick skillet over medium-high heat. Add chicken; cook in 3 batches 3 minutes on each side or until chicken is cooked through. Remove chicken from pan, and keep warm.

3 Combine honey and remaining 5 ingredients in a small bowl; mix well. Add sauce to pan, and cook over medium heat 2 minutes. Spoon sauce over chicken. Reserve 4 chicken cutlets for Dijon Chicken Pizza, if desired.

The Buzz on Honey

There are many types of honey available, and some have strong flavors. Be aware of any flavor intensity when cooking since a honey that's too strong can overwhelm a delicate recipe.

Dijon Chicken Pizza

4 servings

prep: 10 minutes   cook: 10 minutes

⅔   cup pasta sauce

1   (14-ounce) package prebaked Italian
     cheese-flavored pizza bread shell

4   Herbed Dijon Chicken cutlets,
     shredded (opposite page)

1   cup sliced jarred roasted red bell
     peppers

½   cup chopped pitted kalamata olives

½   teaspoon dried oregano

½   cup (2 ounces) shredded mozzarella
     cheese

1 Preheat the oven to 450°. Spread pasta sauce over bread shell, leaving a 1" border. Sprinkle shredded chicken over shell. Top bread with peppers, olives, and oregano; sprinkle with cheese.

2 Place pizza directly on oven rack in center of oven (see tip on page 49). Bake at 450° for 10 minutes or until crust is golden and cheese melts.

"Save the day with this great way to disguise leftovers—a ready-made pizza crust with lots of yummy toppings. It's so easy! And check out my tip on page 49 for how to easily remove a pizza from the oven rack."

Citrus Spice-Drenched Salmon

(pictured on facing page)

4 servings (plus 3 fillets for Salmon Tacos with Tropical Fruit Salsa, page 41)

prep: 15 minutes   cook: 12 minutes

2	tablespoons brown sugar
2	teaspoons salt
1½	teaspoons chili powder
1	teaspoon ground cumin
2	teaspoons grated lemon rind
2	teaspoons grated orange rind
2	teaspoons lemon juice
2	tablespoons olive oil
3	cloves garlic, minced
7	(6-ounce) salmon fillets

Nonstick cooking spray

1 Combine first 9 ingredients in a small bowl. Brush evenly over salmon fillets; let stand 10 minutes.

2 Meanwhile, spray cold grill rack with nonstick cooking spray. Preheat the grill to medium-high heat (350° to 400°).

3 Grill salmon, covered, 5 to 6 minutes on each side or until fish flakes easily with a fork. Reserve 3 fillets for Salmon Tacos with Tropical Fruit Salsa, if desired.

"For an extra splash of citrus, shower your salmon with a squeeze of fresh orange and lemon juices. Ooh it's so fancy!**"**

Frozen Blueberry Margaritas,
page 56

Mango Chutney-Glazed Chicken Skewers,
page 122

Salmon Tacos with Tropical Fruit Salsa

(pictured on facing page)

4 to 8 servings

prep: 11 minutes

1	cup finely chopped pineapple
½	cup finely chopped nectarine or peach
¼	cup finely chopped red bell pepper
1	large jalapeño, seeded and minced
¼	cup finely chopped red onion
2	tablespoons chopped fresh cilantro
¼	cup lime juice

1½	cups angel hair slaw
3	Citrus Spice-Drenched Salmon fillets, cut into chunks and warmed (page 36)
8	taco shells or soft corn tortillas (see note)

1 Combine first 7 ingredients in a small bowl; set aside.

2 Combine slaw and 1 cup fruit salsa in a small bowl; reserve remaining salsa for another use (see tip). Spoon cabbage mixture and salmon evenly into each taco shell. Serve immediately.

Note: If using soft corn tortillas, before filling, place tortillas between 2 paper towels. Microwave at HIGH 30 seconds or until warmed.

"My Tropical Fruit Salsa also does double duty: Serve leftovers with grilled chicken or pork, or scoop up with cinnamon pita chips!**"**

Braised Chicken and Veggies

4 servings (plus 6 chicken thighs and about 3½ cups vegetable mixture for
Creamy Chicken Shepherd's Pie)

prep: 5 minutes   cook: 24 minutes

14	skinned and boned chicken thighs
½	teaspoon salt
¼	teaspoon pepper
¼	cup olive oil, divided
¾	cup all-purpose flour
2¼	cups frozen pearl onions, thawed
2	(8-ounce) packages sliced fresh mushrooms
2	cups chopped carrots
1	cup chopped celery
2	teaspoons prepared minced garlic
1	cup dry white wine or chicken broth
1	(14-ounce) can chicken broth with roasted garlic
¼	cup all-purpose flour

1 Sprinkle chicken thighs evenly with salt and pepper.

2 Heat 2 tablespoons oil in a large Dutch oven over medium-high heat. While pan is heating, dredge chicken thighs in flour. Cook chicken in 2 batches 2 to 3 minutes on each side or until browned. Remove chicken from pan, and set aside.

3 Heat remaining 2 tablespoons oil in Dutch oven; add onions and next 4 ingredients. Cook, covered, 5 minutes or until golden, stirring frequently. Add white wine, scraping bits on bottom of pan with a wooden spoon; return chicken to pan. Combine ½ cup broth and ¼ cup flour; stir well with a whisk to remove lumps. Add flour mixture and remaining broth to Dutch oven.

4 Cover, reduce heat to medium, and simmer 10 minutes or until chicken is done and vegetables are tender. Serve 2 thighs per serving for dinner, and reserve 6 chicken thighs and about 3½ cups vegetable mixture for Creamy Chicken Shepherd's Pie, if desired.

❝*This dish is the ultimate comfort food for my gang! Serve it over warm cooked rice or biscuits for a soul-satisfying meal.*❞

Creamy Chicken Shepherd's Pie

4 servings

prep: 4 minutes   cook: 26 minutes

6   Braised Chicken thighs, chopped
    (opposite page)
3½ cups braised vegetables (from
    Braised Chicken and Veggies,
    opposite page)
1   (1.5-pound) package refrigerated
    mashed potatoes

1 Preheat the oven to 375°. Combine chopped chicken and braised vegetable mixture in a medium microwave-safe bowl. Place chicken mixture and container of mashed potatoes in the microwave; vent the corner of the mashed potatoes. Cook on HIGH 3 minutes or until both chicken mixture and potatoes are warmed.

2 Pour chicken mixture into a lightly greased 2- to 3-quart broiler-proof baking dish. Top evenly with mashed potatoes. Bake at 375° for 18 minutes or until edges are bubbly.

3 Increase oven temperature to broil. Broil 5 minutes or until potatoes are golden.

" *Shepherd's pie is traditionally made with lamb or beef. I put this twist on an old British favorite by using savory chicken thighs.* **"**

Margarita Grilled Pork Tenderloin

4 servings (plus 1 tenderloin for Loaded Cuban Sandwiches)

prep: 5 minutes   cook: 20 minutes   marinate: 8 hours

½   cup frozen limeade concentrate,
      thawed
½   cup water
3   cloves garlic, minced
¼   cup chopped fresh cilantro
1   tablespoon minced jalapeño
1½ tablespoons tequila (optional)
1   teaspoon ground cumin
½   teaspoon chili powder
2   (1-pound) pork tenderloins

Nonstick cooking spray

½   teaspoon salt

1 Combine first 8 ingredients in a large resealable plastic freezer bag. Add pork, and seal; marinate in the refrigerator 8 hours.

2 Spray cold grill rack with nonstick cooking spray. Preheat the grill to medium-high heat (350° to 400°).

3 Remove pork from marinade, discarding marinade. Sprinkle pork evenly with salt. Grill pork, covered, 10 minutes on each side or until a thermometer inserted into thickest part of pork registers 155°. Remove from grill; cover and let stand 5 minutes or until thermometer reaches 160°. Reserve 1 tenderloin for Loaded Cuban Sandwiches, if desired. Cut remaining tenderloin into thin slices to serve.

❝*The marinade in this dish takes only 5 minutes to prepare. Whip up the mixture in the morning, and let the pork marinate throughout the day. Then all you'll need to do is throw the meat on the grill.* **❞**

Loaded Cuban Sandwiches

4 servings

prep: 3 minutes   cook: 4 minutes

4	hoagie rolls
¼	cup Dijon mustard
1	Margarita Grilled Pork Tenderloin, thinly sliced (opposite page)
¼	pound thinly sliced deli ham
8	dill pickle slices
8	slices Swiss cheese

1 Preheat the broiler. Cut a vertical slit down the center of each hoagie roll, leaving ½" of roll attached. Carefully open sides; spread 1 tablespoon mustard on each roll. Top each roll evenly with pork slices, ham, pickles, and cheese.

2 Place open sandwiches on a baking sheet, and broil 3 to 4 minutes or until cheese is melted and bread is golden.

❝Be sure to bring a big appetite to the table when you feast on one of these loaded mile-high sandwiches. It'll definitely hold you over 'til the next meal!❞

Grilled Garlicky Flank Steak

4 servings (plus half of flank steak for Roast Beef & Blue Cheese Panini)

prep: 14 minutes   cook: 16 minutes

Nonstick cooking spray

¼   cup chopped fresh parsley
3   tablespoons minced garlic
1   tablespoon olive oil
½   teaspoon kosher salt
½   teaspoon freshly ground black
      pepper
1   (2-pound) flank steak

Chimichurri (see tip)

1 Spray cold grill rack with nonstick cooking spray. Preheat the grill to medium-high heat (350° to 400°).

2 Combine parsley and next 4 ingredients. Rub mixture evenly over flank steak. Marinate in the refrigerator while preparing Chimichurri.

3 Grill steak, covered, 8 minutes on each side or until desired degree of doneness. Slice steak diagonally across grain into thin slices. Reserve half the slices for Roast Beef & Blue Cheese Panini, if desired. Serve steak with Chimichurri.

Chimichurri

¼   cup olive oil vinaigrette
2   tablespoons chopped fresh parsley
2   tablespoons chopped fresh cilantro
2   tablespoons lemon juice

1 Combine all ingredients in a small bowl. Makes ½ cup

Did You Know?

Chimichurri is a thick Argentinian sauce and marinade for grilled meats. Some large supermarkets carry the sauce in the condiment aisle, so feel free to substitute a prepared brand for the homemade version if it's available in your local store.

Roast Beef & Blue Cheese Panini

4 servings

prep: 10 minutes   cook: 15 minutes

1   tablespoon butter
1   large sweet onion, halved and thinly
       sliced

1   (16-ounce) loaf Italian bread, halved
       lengthwise (such as ciabatta or
       other crusty bread)
2   tablespoons olive oil
½   Grilled Garlicky Flank Steak slices
       (opposite page)
1   cup arugula leaves

4   ounces blue cheese, crumbled
2   tablespoons mayonnaise

1 Preheat the panini grill (see tip). Place butter in a large nonstick skillet over medium-high heat until melted. Add onion slices, and cook 10 minutes or until soft and caramelized, stirring often.

2 Brush outsides of bread with olive oil. Place bottom half of bread on panini grill. Top evenly with steak slices, onion slices, and arugula.

3 Combine blue cheese and mayonnaise; spread mixture on cut side of bread top, and place bread over arugula. Cook 5 minutes or until bread is golden. Slice and serve.

Panini Pressing

An indoor electric grill with a lid works just as well as a panini press for this sandwich. If you don't have either, cook your sandwich on the cooktop in a large skillet, pressing down on the sandwich with another large heavy skillet as it cooks. You'll get the same results.

Kickin' BBQ Chicken

4 servings (plus 2 chicken breasts and ½ cup barbecue sauce for
Cowboy BBQ Chicken Pizza or Loaded BBQ Baked Potato Casserole)

prep: 5 minutes   cook: 24 minutes

Nonstick cooking spray

1   cup ketchup
1   cup spicy, fruity cola (such as
        Dr. Pepper)
¼   cup packed brown sugar
2   tablespoons Worcestershire sauce
1   tablespoon white vinegar
1   tablespoon butter
½   teaspoon garlic powder
½   teaspoon onion powder
½   teaspoon ground red pepper (see tip)

6   (6-ounce) skinned and boned chicken
        breasts

1 Spray cold grill rack with nonstick cooking spray. Preheat the grill to medium-high heat (350° to 400°).

2 Combine ketchup and next 8 ingredients in a medium saucepan. Bring to a boil over medium-high heat; reduce heat to low, and simmer 10 minutes or until thickened.

3 Reserve ½ cup barbecue sauce for Cowboy BBQ Chicken Pizza or Loaded BBQ Baked Potato Casserole, if desired. Brush ½ cup barbecue sauce over chicken. Grill chicken, covered, 5 to 6 minutes on each side or until done, basting with barbecue sauce after first 5 minutes. Reserve 2 chicken breasts for Cowboy BBQ Chicken Pizza or Loaded BBQ Baked Potato Casserole, if desired. Serve grilled chicken with remaining barbecue sauce.

❝ *The sauce on this chicken really packs some heat! If your palate is sensitive, reduce the ground red pepper to tame the flames.* **❞**

Cowboy BBQ Chicken Pizza

4 servings

prep: 10 minutes   cook: 15 minutes

1   (14-ounce) package prebaked Italian
      cheese-flavored pizza bread shell
Nonstick cooking spray

2   Kickin' BBQ Chicken breasts,
      shredded (opposite page)
½   cup barbecue sauce (reserved from
      Kickin' BBQ Chicken, opposite
      page)
1   (7-ounce) can whole kernel corn with
      sweet red bell peppers, drained
½   cup chopped red onion
1½ cups shredded Colby-Cheddar
      cheese
2   tablespoons chopped scallions

1 Preheat the oven to 400°. Spray top
of bread shell with nonstick cooking
spray, and place directly on rack in oven
(see tip). Bake at 400° for 10 minutes or
until golden.

2 Top crust evenly with shredded
chicken; drizzle with barbecue sauce.
Sprinkle evenly with corn, red onion,
and shredded cheese. Bake at 400° for
5 minutes or until cheese is melted and
crust is golden. Top evenly with scallions.

"There will be a stampede for this pizza. Loaded with
color and flavor, it's sure to be a family favorite. You'll be
guaranteed an extra-crispy crust by baking directly on the
oven rack. To easily remove the pizza from the oven, simply slide a large
baking sheet with no sides underneath the crust.**"**

Loaded BBQ Baked Potato Casserole

6 servings

prep: 11 minutes   cook: 19 minutes

6	slices precooked bacon
1	(24-ounce) package refrigerated mashed potatoes
1	cup (4 ounces) shredded Monterey Jack cheese with peppers
½	(8-ounce) package cream cheese, cut into cubes
½	teaspoon salt
½	teaspoon pepper
3	cups (12 ounces) shredded sharp Cheddar cheese, divided
1	(8-ounce) container sour cream
2	Kickin' BBQ Chicken breasts, shredded (page 48)
½	cup barbecue sauce (from Kickin' BBQ Chicken, page 48)

1 Crumble bacon, and set aside. Preheat the oven to 375°.

2 Stir together mashed potatoes, next 4 ingredients, and 2 cups Cheddar cheese in a large microwave-safe bowl. Microwave, covered, at HIGH 4 minutes. Stir in sour cream.

3 Spoon potato mixture into a lightly greased 7" x 11" baking dish. Arrange chicken evenly over potatoes; drizzle with barbecue sauce. Sprinkle evenly with bacon and remaining 1 cup Cheddar cheese.

4 Bake at 375° for 15 minutes or until casserole is thoroughly heated and cheese is melted.

"This dish is a hands-down favorite with my gang! The cheesy casserole is piled high with our favorite baked potato toppings—and then some!"

Snack Attack!

"Quick & easy *are the key words when hunger strikes. So count on these solutions to your hunger dilemma for fast snacks, easy appetizers, and quick beverages.* **"**

Mocha Café au Lait

6 cups

prep: 5 minutes   cook: 8 minutes

2   cups milk
6   ounces milk chocolate candy bars,
        chopped
1½ teaspoons vanilla extract, divided
3   cups freshly brewed coffee

½   cup whipping cream
1   tablespoon confectioners' sugar

1 Stir together milk, chopped chocolate, and 1 teaspoon vanilla in a medium saucepan over low heat. Cook, stirring constantly, 8 minutes or until mixture begins to bubble around edges and chocolate is melted and smooth. Stir in coffee. Remove from heat, and set aside.

2 Beat cream, confectioners' sugar, and remaining ½ teaspoon vanilla at high speed of an electric beater until soft peaks form.

3 Pour hot coffee mixture into mugs. Top with whipped cream.

Chocolate Garnishes

To make 'em, use a mini-grater to grate your favorite dark or milk chocolate bar. Sprinkle over whipped cream to garnish this or any of your favorite beverages.

Hot Mulled Cider

7½ cups

prep: 10 minutes   cook: 1 hour

2   quarts apple cider
½   cup packed light brown sugar

1   teaspoon whole allspice
½   teaspoon whole cloves
2   (3") cinnamon sticks
1   orange, peeled and sliced

1 Stir together apple cider and brown sugar in a Dutch oven.

2 Combine allspice, cloves, and cinnamon sticks in a small piece of cheesecloth, and tie with kitchen twine. Add spice bag and orange slices to cider.

3 Simmer over low heat 1 hour. Remove spice bag and oranges before serving.

"*This cider takes only 10 minutes to mix together. While it simmers, you can be getting food ready for a party or simply enjoying the fragrant aroma that fills up your house.***"**

Chocolate Eggnog

9½ cups

prep: 15 minutes

1	quart refrigerated eggnog
1	quart milk
1	(16-ounce) can chocolate syrup
½	cup light rum (optional)
1	cup whipping cream
2	tablespoons confectioners' sugar

Unsweetened cocoa (optional)

1 Stir together first 3 ingredients and, if desired, rum in a punch bowl, stirring well.

2 Beat whipping cream at high speed of an electric beater until foamy. Add confectioners' sugar, beating until medium peaks form. Dollop whipped cream over individual servings. Sift cocoa over whipped cream, if desired.

"Store-bought eggnog is elevated to new heights with the addition of chocolate syrup and whipped cream. Yum-my!**"**

Cranberry Lemonade

8 cups

prep: 10 minutes

5   cups water, divided
½   cup sugar

1   (6-ounce) can frozen lemonade
        concentrate, thawed
3   cups cranberry juice

1 Stir together 2 cups water and the sugar in a small saucepan over medium heat, stirring until sugar dissolves.

2 Stir together sugar mixture, thawed lemonade concentrate, cranberry juice, and remaining 3 cups water. Chill until ready to serve.

"This simple sipper will quench your thirst during the dog days of summer or any ol' time of the year!"

Frozen Blueberry Margaritas

(pictured on page 38)

5½ cups

prep: 15 minutes

Fresh orange juice or lime juice (optional)
Decorator sugar crystals (optional)

3   cups ice
⅓   cup tequila
2   cups fresh or frozen blueberries
1   (6-ounce) can frozen limeade
       concentrate
¼   cup confectioners' sugar
¼   cup orange liqueur

1 Dip rims of margarita glasses in orange juice then dip in sugar crystals to coat, if desired.

2 Process ice and remaining 5 ingredients in a blender until smooth. Serve in prepared glasses.

"Blueberries have amazing health benefits—they're one of the top sources of disease-fighting antioxidants in fruits and vegetables. So, cheers to good health!"

Fizzy Raspberry Lemonade

7 cups

prep: 10 minutes

1 (12-ounce) can frozen lemonade
   concentrate, thawed and undiluted
1 (10-ounce) package frozen
   raspberries, partially thawed
   (see tip)
3 tablespoons sugar

1 (1-liter) bottle club soda, chilled

1 Process first 3 ingredients in a blender until smooth, stopping to scrape down sides.

2 Pour raspberry mixture through a wire-mesh strainer into a large pitcher, discarding seeds; stir in club soda. Serve over ice.

Fizzy Strawberry Lemonade

For a strawberry twist, substitute a 10-ounce package of frozen strawberries, partially thawed, for frozen raspberries. Prepare recipe as directed.

Apple Spice-Raisin Snack Mix

about 6 cups

prep: 10 minutes   cook: 14 minutes

3	cups whole-grain oat cereal squares
1	tablespoon sugar
2	teaspoons apple pie spice

Nonstick cooking spray

1	(11.5-ounce) can dry-roasted mixed nuts
1	cup raisins

1 Preheat the oven to 350°. Combine first 3 ingredients in a medium bowl. Coat cereal mixture evenly with nonstick cooking spray. Transfer to an aluminum foil-lined rimmed baking sheet coated with cooking spray.

2 Bake at 350° for 7 minutes. Stir mixture, and coat evenly with cooking spray. Bake 7 more minutes. Stir in nuts and raisins; cool. Store mixture in an airtight container.

"*Stash this snack in the pantry for a quick pick-me-up, or pack it for a snack-on-the-go. Either way, it's a healthy treat!***"**

Fancy Schmancy G.O.R.P.

8 cups

prep: 5 minutes

1   (16-ounce) package candy-coated
      chocolate pieces
1   (12-ounce) jar unsalted roasted
      peanuts
1   (6-ounce) can salted natural almonds
1   (6-ounce) package semisweet
      chocolate chips
1   (6-ounce) package butterscotch chips
1   cup raisins

1 Combine all ingredients in a large
bowl, stirring gently; store in an airtight container.

"G.O.R.P. *stands for a snack mix of 'Good Old Raisins
and Peanuts.' It has grown to include everything from nuts
and raisins to seeds, dried fruit, and toasted oats. I added
my spin to this traditional energy booster with the addition of chocolate
and butterscotch chips and chocolate candies! Betcha can't wait to get a
handful of these goodies!***"**

Pop Graham Munchies

about 12 cups

prep: 5 minutes   cook: 25 minutes

10   cups popped popcorn
3   cups honey graham cereal
2   cups miniature marshmallows
1½   cups golden raisins

½   cup butter
¼   cup packed brown sugar
1½   teaspoons ground cinnamon
¼   teaspoon ground ginger
¼   teaspoon ground nutmeg

1 Preheat oven to 325°. Combine first 4 ingredients in a large roasting pan. Set aside.

2 Combine butter and remaining 4 ingredients in a small saucepan; cook over low heat, stirring constantly, until butter melts. Pour over popcorn mixture, tossing to coat.

3 Bake at 325° for 20 minutes, stirring every 5 minutes. Pour onto wax paper, and break apart into clumps as mixture cools. Store in an airtight container.

❝ *Kids of all ages will clamor to get their hands on this tasty snack. It makes a great gift as well!* **❞**

Toffee Apple Dip

about 3 cups

prep: 5 minutes

1   (8-ounce) package cream cheese,
    softened
1   (8-ounce) package toffee bits
¾   cup packed light brown sugar
½   cup granulated sugar
1   teaspoon vanilla extract

1 Stir together all ingredients in a medium bowl until well blended. Serve immediately, or store in an airtight container in the refrigerator up to 5 days.

Twice as Good

One recipe makes enough dip for serving with 6 large apples or pears. To prevent the cut fruit from turning brown, soak the slices for an hour in canned pineapple juice.

Also try spreading this creamy mixture over the top of a chocolate sheet cake. It doesn't get as firm as a traditional frosting, so store the cake in the refrigerator.

Quick Fiesta Dip

1½ cups

prep: 5 minutes   cook: 7 minutes

1   (9-ounce) package frozen corn
      niblets

1   (12-ounce) jar thick-and-chunky mild
      salsa

1   cup (4 ounces) shredded Colby or
      Cheddar cheese

1 Cook corn according to package
directions; drain.

2 Pour salsa into a 9" microwave-safe
glass pie plate; stir in corn. Cover
with plastic wrap; fold back a small section of wrap to allow steam to escape.
Microwave at HIGH 2 minutes or until
bubbly.

3 Sprinkle cheese over salsa; cover with
plastic wrap. Let stand 5 minutes or
until cheese is melted. Serve with tortilla
or corn chips.

"_Three ingredients are all it takes to whip_
up this fast, flavorful snack!**"**

Layered Spicy Black Bean Dip

8 appetizer servings

prep: 10 minutes

1   (8-ounce) package cream cheese,
      softened
1   (16-ounce) jar spicy black bean dip
½   (8-ounce) package shredded Mexican
      cheese blend
Toppings: sliced scallions, chopped
      tomatoes, sliced ripe black olives

1 Layer cream cheese, dip, and cheese in a 1-quart serving dish. Add toppings, and serve with tortilla and corn chips.

"*This easy-to-make dip can be put together in 10 minutes! Keep the ingredients on hand for drop-in guests, or make the dip ahead when you're expecting the gang!***"**

Italian Brie

8 appetizer servings

prep: 5 minutes

1   (8-ounce) round Brie
1   (3.5-ounce) jar prepared pesto
½   cup sun-dried tomatoes in oil,
        drained and chopped

1 Trim and discard rind from top of Brie. Place Brie on a serving plate; spread top with pesto, and sprinkle with chopped tomatoes.

"*Serve this savory appetizer with black olives and baguette slices or crackers. Magnifico!***"**

Swiss 'n' Walnut Pears

5 appetizer servings

prep: 15 minutes   cook: 3 minutes

⅓   cup finely chopped walnuts

1   pear (*see tip*)
3   (¾-ounce) wedges Swiss
       spreadable cheese

1 Heat walnuts in a small nonstick skillet over medium-low heat 2 to 3 minutes or until toasted, stirring often.

2 Cut pear into about 20 equal slices. Stir together cheese wedges. Spread bottom half of 1 side of each pear slice evenly with cheese. Sprinkle with walnuts.

"Impress 'em with this 3-ingredient winner. The flavors and textures of the ingredients pair perfectly. I like to use a Bosc or Bartlett pear for this tasty snack."

Simple Antipasto Platter

8 appetizer servings

prep: 10 minutes

1	(4-ounce) log goat cheese
2	tablespoons chopped fresh parsley

1	(16-ounce) jar pickled okra, drained
1	(10-ounce) jar pitted kalamata olives, rinsed and drained
1	(7-ounce) jar roasted red bell peppers, drained and cut into strips
1	(4-ounce) package sliced salami

Assorted crackers and breadsticks

1 Roll goat cheese log in parsley to coat evenly; place on a serving platter.

2 Arrange okra and next 3 ingredients on platter around goat cheese. Serve with crackers and breadsticks.

"If you can open a jar, you can arrange this platter. Simply roll a log of goat cheese in chopped fresh parsley then just arrange these or your other favorite antipasto items around it for an effortless and tasty party offering."

Hot Dog Pizzas

10 servings

prep: 5 minutes   cook: 10 minutes

1   (12-ounce) can refrigerated
       buttermilk biscuits

¼   cup mayonnaise
¼   teaspoon garlic powder
1¼   cups (5 ounces) shredded mozzarella
       cheese, divided
3   frankfurters, sliced

1 Preheat oven to 400°. Separate biscuits, and press each into a 4" circle on lightly greased baking sheets.

2 Combine mayonnaise and garlic powder; brush evenly over biscuit rounds. Sprinkle ¾ cup cheese evenly over mayonnaise mixture, and top with frankfurter slices.

3 Bake at 400° for 5 minutes; sprinkle with remaining ½ cup cheese, and bake 5 more minutes or until lightly browned and cheese melts. Serve immediately.

"*Two childhood favorites (and favorites of some adults I know) come together in one terrific snack. Be sure to keep the ingredients on hand for the after-school crowd.***"**

Spicy Chipotle-Barbecue Sausage Bites

12 appetizer servings

prep: 5 minutes   cook: 20 minutes

1   (28-ounce) bottle barbecue sauce
1   (18-ounce) jar cherry preserves
3   canned chipotle peppers in adobo
     sauce, undrained and chopped
½   cup water
1   tablespoon adobo sauce from can

2   (16-ounce) packages cocktail-size
     smoked sausages (see tip)

1 Whisk together first 5 ingredients in a Dutch oven over medium-high heat.

2 Bring mixture to a boil; add sausages, and return to a boil. Reduce heat to medium, and simmer 15 minutes, stirring occasionally. Keep warm in a slow cooker on LOW setting, if desired.

Spicy Chipotle-Barbecue Meatballs
Substitute a 32-ounce package of frozen meatballs for the sausages, and increase the water to 1½ cups. Proceed as directed above, increasing the simmer time to 45 minutes. This version makes the same number of servings.

Kick-Off Beef Pretzel Poppers

6 to 8 appetizer servings

prep: 15 minutes

½ (8-ounce) container soft cream
cheese
½ cup (2 ounces) finely shredded sharp
Cheddar cheese
½ to 1 tablespoon minced pickled
jalapeño pepper slices (see note)
Pinch of garlic powder

20 thinly sliced deli roast beef slices
20 (3") honey wheat pretzel sticks

1 Stir together first 4 ingredients in a small bowl until well blended.

2 Spread about 1 teaspoon cream cheese mixture on 1 side of each roast beef slice; top each slice with 1 pretzel stick, and roll up. Serve immediately, or chill up to 1 hour.

Note: Presliced jalapeño peppers can be found in cans in the Mexican food section of your supermarket or pickled in jars in the condiment section.

Horseradish-Dijon Pretzel Poppers
Mix up this recipe a bit by omitting the shredded Cheddar, jalapeño pepper slices, and garlic powder. Instead, stir together the cream cheese with 1 tablespoon finely chopped scallions, ½ teaspoon prepared horseradish, and 2 teaspoons Dijon mustard. Then proceed with the recipe as directed above.

Chili-Cheese Quesadillas

8 appetizer servings

prep: 15 minutes   cook: 8 minutes

1   (3-ounce) package cream cheese,
      softened
1   cup (4 ounces) shredded American
      cheese
1   cup (4 ounces) shredded Cheddar
      cheese
1   (4.5-ounce) can chopped green
      chilies
¼   teaspoon garlic powder
⅛   teaspoon ground red pepper
8   (8") flour tortillas

1 Beat first 6 ingredients at medium speed of an electric beater until well blended. Spread about ½ cup cheese mixture onto each of 4 tortillas, leaving a ½" border. Top with remaining tortillas.

2 Heat a lightly greased large nonstick skillet over medium-high heat. Cook quesadillas in 4 batches 1 minute on each side or until filling melts and outside browns. Cut into wedges to serve. Serve with sour cream and salsa, if desired.

❝Let the gang share in the fun of making a steady supply of warm quesadillas at your next fiesta.**❞**

Breakfasts & Brunches

"Jump-start your morning the right way with breakfast! Whether it's a breakfast-on-the-run or a leisurely brunch, you'll get all the fuel you'll need—and fast—with these morning delights. After all, breakfast is the most important meal of the day. Rise and shine!"

Healthful Granola

5 cups

prep: 5 minutes   cook: 20 minutes

2	cups uncooked regular oats
¾	cup uncooked hot oat bran cereal
½	cup sliced almonds
1	teaspoon ground cinnamon
¼	teaspoon salt
½	cup honey
2	tablespoons vegetable oil
1	tablespoon water
½	teaspoon vanilla extract
¾	cup raisins
½	cup chopped pitted dates
⅓	cup dried cranberries
¼	cup sunflower kernels

1 Preheat the oven to 350°. Combine first 5 ingredients in a large bowl.

2 Stir together honey and next 3 ingredients in a small bowl; stir into dry ingredients. Spread mixture onto a 10" x 15" rimmed baking sheet.

3 Bake at 350° for 20 minutes or until dark brown, stirring often; cool in pan on a wire rack. Stir in raisins and remaining ingredients, and store in an airtight container. Stir granola into yogurt, or sprinkle over cereal.

"*This granola is not only good for you, it's good to eat! Keep it on hand for healthy—and tasty—snacking for kids and grown-ups alike.***"**

Layered Strawberry-Ginger Yogurt Cups

4 servings

prep: 9 minutes

2 cups plain Greek yogurt (see tip)
2 cups strawberries, sliced
¼ cup crushed toffee bits
¼ cup finely minced crystallized ginger

1 Spoon ¼ cup yogurt into each of 4 (6-ounce) stemmed glasses; top with half the strawberry slices. Sprinkle with half each of the toffee bits and ginger. Repeat layers.

It's Greek to Me

Because Greek yogurt is strained, it has a thicker, more velvety texture than regular yogurt. Look for the Greek variety in the organic section of your supermarket. If you can't find it, just substitute sour cream.

Spiced Fruit Salad

2¼ cups

prep: 3 minutes   cook: 8 minutes   chill: 8 hours

¼   cup sugar
¼   cup water
2   star anise (see tip)
1   orange-and-spice tea bag

1   cup fresh orange sections
1   cup fresh grapefruit sections
1   cup cubed fresh pineapple

1 Bring first 3 ingredients to a boil in a small saucepan; boil, stirring constantly, until sugar dissolves. Remove from heat, and add tea bag; cover and steep 5 minutes. Remove tea bag, squeezing gently. Cool.

2 Remove and discard star anise. Toss together fruit and tea mixture. Cover and chill 8 hours.

Star Anise
It's shaped like an 8-pointed star and imparts licorice flavor to this fresh fruit salad. Look for star anise in the spice section of your supermarket.

Cinnamon-Walnut-Cherry Oatmeal

4 servings

prep: 2 minutes   cook: 12 minutes

2   cups milk
1½ cups water
⅓   cup dried cherries

2   cups quick-cooking oats
1   teaspoon ground cinnamon
½   teaspoon salt
3   tablespoons maple syrup

½   cup chopped walnuts, toasted

1 Combine milk, water, and dried cherries in a large saucepan; bring just to a boil over medium heat.

2 Add oats, cinnamon, and salt to saucepan; reduce heat to medium-low, and simmer, stirring constantly, 2 to 3 minutes or until thickened. Stir in maple syrup.

3 Spoon oatmeal into bowls; sprinkle with walnuts.

"I love this welcome change from sugary-sweet oatmeal! But if you wake up with a sweet tooth, simply increase the amount of maple syrup you use as desired."

South-of-the-Border Eggs

4 servings

prep: 5 minutes   cook: 25 minutes

1   tablespoon olive oil, divided
2   medium zucchini, sliced
½   teaspoon salt, divided
¼   teaspoon pepper, divided

4   (6") corn tortillas
4   large eggs

¾   cup (3 ounces) shredded Monterey
        Jack cheese with peppers
Toppings: fresh salsa, chopped cilantro,
        avocado slices

1 Heat 1 teaspoon oil in a large non-stick skillet over medium-high heat. Add zucchini, and sauté 8 minutes or until golden. Sprinkle with ¼ teaspoon salt and ⅛ teaspoon pepper; remove from skillet, and keep warm.

2 In the same skillet, heat tortillas, 2 at a time, for 2 minutes on each side (see tip). Remove from skillet, and keep warm. Heat 1 teaspoon olive oil in the skillet; add 2 eggs, and sprinkle evenly with ⅛ teaspoon salt and dash of pepper. Fry to desired degree of doneness, turning once. Repeat with remaining olive oil, eggs, salt, and pepper.

3 Place toasted tortillas on serving plates; top evenly with zucchini, cheese, and eggs. Serve with desired toppings.

"*Don't be tempted to walk away when toasting the tortillas for this recipe—they become golden and crispy very quickly!***"**

Antipasto Frittata

4 to 6 servings

prep: 5 minutes   cook: 10 minutes

6   large eggs
½   cup half-and-half
¼   cup shredded Parmesan cheese
¼   teaspoon salt
¼   teaspoon pepper

1½   tablespoons extra virgin olive oil
2   ounces thinly sliced Genoa salami,
        cut into ½" pieces
1   (14-ounce) can quartered artichoke
        hearts, drained and chopped
½   cup whole milk ricotta cheese
1   cup (4 ounces) shredded Italian
        cheese blend

1 Preheat the broiler. Whisk together first 5 ingredients in a large bowl.

2 Heat olive oil in an 8" to 8½" non-stick, ovenproof skillet over medium heat on the stovetop. Pour egg mixture into skillet; sprinkle evenly with salami and chopped artichokes. Cover and cook 5 to 6 minutes or until eggs are set around the edges but still moist in the center. Uncover and drop ricotta cheese by teaspoonfuls over egg mixture; sprinkle with shredded cheese. Broil 3" from heat 4 minutes or until eggs are set and top is golden.

3 Using a flexible spatula, loosen frittata around edges, and slide onto a serving platter. Cut into wedges. Serve hot or at room temperature.

Did You Know?

A frittata is an Italian omelet that resembles a crustless quiche. But it's different from an omelet in that it's finished under a broiler, cut into wedges to serve, and not folded during the cooking process.

Mushroom, Bacon, Swiss Breakfast Calzones

4 servings

prep: 8 minutes   cook: 22 minutes

1	tablespoon olive oil
1	(12-ounce) package sliced mushrooms
¼	teaspoon salt
⅛	teaspoon ground black pepper
1	(13.8-ounce) can refrigerated pizza dough
8	slices fully cooked bacon, crumbled
1	cup (4 ounces) shredded Swiss cheese

Nonstick cooking spray

1 Preheat the oven to 400°. Heat oil in a large skillet over medium-high heat. Add mushrooms; sauté 7 minutes or until liquid is almost absorbed. Stir in salt and pepper.

2 Unroll dough, and pat into a 10" x 14" rectangle. Cut dough into quarters to form four 5" x 7" rectangles. Arrange mushrooms and bacon on half of one short end of rectangles to within ½" of edges; sprinkle with cheese.

3 Fold remaining halves of dough over filling, pressing edges firmly to seal. Place on a baking sheet coated with nonstick cooking spray. Spray tops of dough with cooking spray. Bake at 400° for 13 minutes or until golden.

"Calzones in the morning? You betcha! They're great for breakfast-on-the-go or for brunch. And since they're little rectangles, they're easy to handle—and eat.**"**

Breakfast Burritos

4 servings

prep: 5 minutes   cook: 13 minutes

½   pound hot or mild ground pork
      sausage
1   tablespoon taco seasoning mix
      (see tip)
6   large eggs, lightly beaten

½   cup (2 ounces) shredded Mexican
      four-cheese blend

4   burrito-size flour tortillas
Salsa

1 Cook sausage and taco seasoning mix in a nonstick skillet over medium heat, stirring until the sausage crumbles and is no longer pink. Add eggs, and cook, without stirring, until eggs begin to set on bottom. Draw a spatula across bottom of pan to form large curds. Continue to cook until eggs are thickened but still moist, about 5 minutes.

2 Sprinkle eggs evenly with cheese. Turn off heat, and cover. Let stand 5 minutes or until cheese melts.

3 Spoon mixture evenly into tortillas, roll up tightly, and serve with salsa.

Waste Not!
Toss the remaining 2 tablespoons of taco seasoning mix from the packet into 2 (1.5-ounce) bags of popped microwave popcorn for a zippy snack.

Creole Breakfast Crostinis

4 servings

prep: 20 minutes   cook: 5 minutes

1   (11-ounce) package meatless
      breakfast starters scramble
4   large eggs
¾   teaspoon Creole seasoning

½   (8-ounce) French bread baguette
4   (1-ounce) slices Monterey Jack
      cheese with peppers

1   (1.25-ounce) envelope hollandaise
      sauce mix
1   tablespoon Creole mustard
1   teaspoon dried parsley
¼   teaspoon ground red pepper

1 Preheat the oven to 400°. Prepare breakfast starters with eggs according to package directions, adding the Creole seasoning.

2 Cut bread diagonally into 4 (1¼"-thick) slices. Top bread slices with cheese, and place on a baking sheet.

3 Bake at 400° for 5 minutes or until cheese is melted and bread is lightly toasted.

4 Meanwhile, prepare hollandaise sauce mix according to package directions. Stir in mustard and remaining 2 ingredients. Top bread slices evenly with scrambled egg mixture. Drizzle evenly with Creole mustard mixture. Serve immediately.

This breakfast eye-opener can be made with either traditional eggs or egg substitute—it's delicious with either one. I like serving any extra Creole mustard mixture with fresh tomato slices (my favorite!) or over blanched asparagus and green beans.

Sausage-Filled Crêpes

6 to 8 servings

prep: 5 minutes   cook: 25 minutes

1	pound ground pork sausage
1	small onion, diced
2	cups (8 ounces) shredded Cheddar cheese, divided
1	(3-ounce) package cream cheese
½	teaspoon dried marjoram
12	(9") refrigerated ready-to-use crêpes (see tip)
½	cup sour cream
¼	cup butter, softened
¼	cup chopped fresh parsley or 1 tablespoon dried parsley

1 Preheat the oven to 350°. Cook sausage and onion in a large skillet over medium heat, stirring until the sausage crumbles and is no longer pink; drain sausage well.

2 Return sausage to skillet; add 1 cup Cheddar cheese, the cream cheese, and marjoram, stirring until cheeses melt.

3 Spoon 3 tablespoons filling down center of each crêpe. Roll up, and place seam-side down in a lightly greased 9" x 13" baking dish. Bake, covered, at 350° for 15 minutes.

4 Stir together sour cream and butter; spoon over crêpes. Bake 5 more minutes. Sprinkle with remaining 1 cup Cheddar cheese and the parsley.

Plan Ahead

You can find refrigerated ready-to-use crêpes in the produce section of most supermarkets. These sausage-filled crêpes may be assembled and frozen up to a month in an airtight container. To reheat, let stand for 30 minutes at room temperature. Bake, covered, at 350° for 40 minutes. Proceed as directed.

Chorizo Fajitas

4 servings

prep: 7 minutes   cook: 14 minutes

1 tablespoon vegetable oil
1 large onion, thinly sliced

8 ounces soft chorizo (see tip)
1 large red bell pepper, thinly sliced
1 large green bell pepper, thinly sliced

8 (8") flour tortillas, warmed
4 large eggs, scrambled (optional)
1½ cups (6 ounces) shredded Mexican
    cheese blend
Toppings: salsa, sour cream, fresh
    chopped cilantro

1 Heat oil in a large nonstick skillet over medium-high heat. Add onion, and sauté 5 minutes or until golden.

2 Remove and discard chorizo casings. Add chorizo and peppers to skillet; cook 5 to 6 minutes, stirring until the chorizo crumbles and browns. Drain well.

3 Spoon chorizo mixture down the center of each tortilla; top with eggs, if desired, and cheese. Fold sides in, and roll up burrito-style. Serve with desired toppings.

What Is Chorizo?

This traditional ingredient in Mexican and Spanish dishes is a spicy pork sausage that's seasoned with garlic and chili powder. There are usually two types of chorizo sold in supermarkets: One is labeled "smoked and dried" and is hard like pepperoni. The other is slightly softer. With both types, be sure to remove the casings before browning.

Breakfast Pizza

3 to 4 servings

prep: 2 minutes   cook: 15 minutes

1   (14-ounce) package prebaked Italian
       pizza bread shell
1   cup (4 ounces) shredded gourmet
       three-cheese blend
8   bacon slices, cooked and crumbled

2   large eggs
½   cup milk

1 Preheat the oven to 400°. Place bread shell on a baking sheet, and sprinkle with shredded cheese and bacon.

2 Whisk together eggs and milk until well blended; pour over center of bread shell. Bake at 400° for 12 to 15 minutes or until egg mixture is set and cheese is golden. Cut into wedges, and serve immediately.

Have It Your Way

Try chopped cooked ham or chicken, crumbled cooked sausage, or chopped vegetables on the pizza, too. Just add the desired toppings to the bread shell before you pour the egg mixture on top.

Shrimp and "Grits"

3 to 4 servings

prep: 4 minutes   cook: 13 minutes

4   slices bacon

1   (16-ounce) tube plain polenta
        (see tip)
½   cup water
1   cup (8 ounces) shredded sharp
        Cheddar cheese

¾   pound frozen peeled and deveined,
        medium-sized uncooked shrimp,
        thawed
1   teaspoon minced garlic
½   cup thinly sliced scallions
1   tablespoon lemon juice
½   teaspoon hot sauce

1 Cook bacon in a large skillet over medium-high heat until crisp; remove bacon, and drain on paper towels, reserving drippings in skillet. Crumble bacon.

2 Meanwhile, mash polenta and water in a medium saucepan. Cook over low heat until hot, stirring occasionally. Add cheese, and stir until melted.

3 Heat drippings in skillet over medium-high heat. Pat shrimp dry; add to skillet with garlic and scallions. Sauté 3 minutes or just until shrimp turn pink. Stir in lemon juice; cook 20 seconds. Stir in hot sauce.

4 To serve, spoon polenta mixture onto serving plates; top with shrimp mixture, and sprinkle with bacon.

"Polenta is just the fancy schmancy Italian version of grits. You can find tubes of refrigerated pre-cooked polenta in the produce section of most supermarkets.**"**

Hot Chocolate Muffins

1 dozen

prep: 8 minutes   cook: 12 minutes

2¼ cups biscuit baking mix
½   cup sugar
2   tablespoons unsweetened cocoa

½   cup half-and-half
¼   cup chocolate syrup
3   tablespoons vegetable oil
2   teaspoons vanilla extract
1   large egg, lightly beaten
¾   cup mini semisweet chocolate chips
¼   cup sliced almonds

1 Preheat the oven to 400°. Combine baking mix, sugar, and cocoa in a large bowl. Make a well in center of mixture.

2 Combine half-and-half and next 4 ingredients in a small bowl; add to dry ingredients, stirring just until dry ingredients are moistened. Stir in chocolate chips and almonds.

3 Spoon into greased muffin pans, filling two-thirds full. Bake at 400° for 11 to 12 minutes or until a wooden toothpick inserted in center comes out clean. Remove from pans immediately.

"Two favorites, chocolate and homemade bread, mix together in this delicious muffin recipe. I bet these won't last long around your house!**"**

Banana Pancakes with Golden Banana Syrup

(pictured on page 107)

12 (4") pancakes

prep: 12 minutes   cook: 9 minutes

3   large bananas, divided
⅔   cup maple or pancake syrup
2   tablespoons butter

2   large eggs
1   tablespoon sugar
⅔   cup milk
2   cups biscuit baking mix

Butter-flavored nonstick cooking spray

1 Peel and cut 2 bananas into ¼"-thick slices. Combine syrup and butter in a medium saucepan; bring to a simmer. Stir in sliced bananas, and remove from heat.

2 Mash remaining banana in a medium bowl; whisk in eggs, sugar, and milk. Whisk in baking mix until blended.

3 Pour about ¼ cup batter for each pancake onto a hot griddle coated with nonstick cooking spray. Cook pancakes until tops are covered with bubbles; turn and cook other side of pancakes. Repeat procedure with remaining pancake batter. Serve pancakes with banana syrup.

❝*There's no monkeying around when I say that I'm bananas over these pancakes! And you're gonna love how you get 'em—the bananas—in each bite of pancake and in the syrup. Fire up the griddle now!***❞**

Baked Pancake with Glazed Apples

4 servings

prep: 2 minutes   cook: 23 minutes

2   tablespoons butter

½   cup milk
2   large eggs
6   tablespoons all-purpose flour
1   tablespoon sugar
⅛   teaspoon salt

1   (12-ounce) package frozen apples

1 Preheat the oven to 425°. Place butter in a 10" cast iron skillet; place in the oven for 6 minutes or until sizzling.

2 Meanwhile, combine milk and next 4 ingredients in a large bowl; beat well with a wire whisk. Remove skillet from oven; pour batter into skillet. Bake at 425° for 17 minutes or until pancake is puffed, golden, and set.

3 While pancake bakes, prepare apples according to package directions. To serve, cut pancake into wedges, and serve with warm apples.

"You may have heard a baked pancake referred to as a Dutch baby. Whichever name you prefer, be sure to serve the dish hot out of the oven before it deflates.**"**

Ham-and-Cheese Oven French Toast

6 servings

prep: 10 minutes   cook: 20 minutes

12   sandwich bread slices
¼   cup prepared mustard
12   (1-ounce) baked ham slices
6   (1-ounce) Monterey Jack cheese
      slices

3   large eggs
½   cup milk

1 Preheat the oven to 475°. Spread 1 side of each bread slice with mustard. Layer 6 bread slices mustard-side up with 1 ham slice, 1 cheese slice, and another ham slice; top with remaining bread slices, mustard-side down.

2 Whisk together eggs and milk in a shallow dish until blended. Dip each sandwich into egg mixture, coating both sides.

3 Place sandwiches 2" apart on a lightly greased baking sheet. Place another lightly greased baking sheet greased-side down on top of sandwiches. Bake at 475° for 15 to 20 minutes or until golden brown. Serve immediately.

"Skipping breakfast isn't an option when this hearty French toast is on the menu! Just add O.J., and you're set.**"**

French Toast Bread Pudding

6 servings

prep: 6 minutes   cook: 20 minutes

1   (16-ounce) box frozen French toast
      sticks
¼   cup raisins

2   large eggs
3   cups milk
½   cup sugar
1   teaspoon vanilla extract
2   tablespoons light brown sugar

Maple or pancake syrup

1 Preheat the oven to 425°. Cut bread sticks crosswise into 1" pieces. Place bread cubes in a lightly greased 9" x 13" baking dish; sprinkle raisins evenly over bread cubes.

2 Whisk together eggs and next 3 ingredients in a medium bowl. Pour egg mixture evenly over bread. Press bread to absorb mixture. Sprinkle brown sugar evenly over bread.

3 Bake at 425° for 20 minutes. Serve with syrup.

❝*This treat is a hands-down winner with the kids in my family!*❞

Super Breakfast Sundaes

4 servings

prep: 15 minutes

4   frozen toaster waffles

2   bananas, sliced
2   (8-ounce) containers lemon yogurt
1   cup sliced fresh strawberries
1   cup fresh blueberries
½   cup toasted oat O-shaped cereal
Strawberry syrup (see note)

1 Cook waffles according to package directions. Cut into quarters.

2 Place banana slices evenly in 4 serving glasses or bowls. Layer evenly with half each of the yogurt, berries, and cereal. Repeat layers once. Top with waffle quarters. Serve with syrup.

Note: Look for strawberry syrup with the ice cream toppings.

"You'll get requests for these sundaes all week long! How can you resist giving in when they're loaded with fresh fruit? Feel free to use any fruit-flavored yogurt."

Good for You!

"Take a healthier approach to weeknight favorites with these enticing dishes, from scrumptious desserts to mouthwatering entrées. Healthy and quick food is food that's oh-so-good for you!**"**

Raisin Brownie Bars

16 bars

prep: 5 minutes   cook: 25 minutes

⅔ cup all-purpose flour
1   cup sugar
½   cup unsweetened cocoa
½   teaspoon baking powder
3   tablespoons butter, melted
1   large egg
1   large egg white
½   cup milk chocolate-covered raisins

Nonstick cooking spray

1 Preheat the oven to 350°. Combine flour and next 6 ingredients in a medium bowl, stirring until dry ingredients are moistened (mixture will be thick). Let mixture stand 10 minutes. Fold in chocolate-covered raisins.

2 Press mixture into an 8" square pan coated with nonstick cooking spray. Bake at 350° for 23 to 25 minutes. Cool in pan on a wire rack.

Per bar: CALORIES 123 (27% from fat); FAT 3.7g (sat 2.1g); PROTEIN 1.9g; CARBOHYDRATE 22.1g; FIBER 0.8g; CHOLESTEROL 19mg; IRON 0.5mg; SODIUM 38mg; CALCIUM 17mg

"If you're craving chocolate, these dark, fudgy brownies are the ticket! The mixture is very thick and requires a standing time of 10 minutes. Don't skimp on this—it gives the dry ingredients time to moisten, and the wait is definitely worth it!"

Cocoa-Cranberry Crispy Bars

2 dozen

prep: 7 minutes   cook: 3 minutes

1   (10-ounce) package large
      marshmallows
2   tablespoons butter

6   cups chocolate-flavored oven-toasted
      rice cereal
1   cup sweetened dried cranberries or
      raisins
½   cup mini semisweet chocolate chips

Nonstick cooking spray

1 Combine marshmallows and butter in a large microwave-safe bowl. Microwave at HIGH 2 minutes. Stir well; microwave 1 more minute.

2 Combine cereal, cranberries, and chocolate chips in a large bowl. Pour marshmallow mixture over cereal mixture, stirring until combined.

3 Press cereal mixture into a 9" x 13" baking dish coated with nonstick cooking spray. Cool completely; cut into bars.

Per bar: CALORIES 118 (18% from fat); FAT 2.4g (sat 1.5g); PROTEIN 0.8g; CARBOHYDRATE 24.7g; FIBER 0.6g; CHOLESTEROL 3mg; IRON 0.8mg; SODIUM 76mg; CALCIUM 3mg

No-Stick Solution
Coat your spoon with nonstick cooking spray before stirring the cereal into the marshmallow mixture. It'll keep the cereal from sticking to the spoon.

Key Lime-Strawberry Tarts

6 tarts

prep: 10 minutes   chill: 30 minutes

½ (14-ounce) can fat-free sweetened
    condensed milk (about ½ cup)
¼ cup Key lime juice
¾ cup plus 2 tablespoons frozen
    fat-free whipped topping, thawed
    and divided

6 (3") graham cracker tart shells
12 strawberries, sliced

1 Whisk together condensed milk, lime juice, and ½ cup whipped topping in a small bowl.

2 Pour filling evenly into tart shells. Cover and chill 30 minutes or until ready to serve. Top tarts evenly with strawberries and remaining whipped topping.

Per tart: CALORIES 227 (24% from fat); FAT 6.1g (sat 1g); PROTEIN 3.7g; CARBOHYDRATE 38.4g; FIBER 1.5g; CHOLESTEROL 4mg; IRON 0.5mg; SODIUM 184mg; CALCIUM 89mg

The Key to Limes

A Key lime is smaller and has a thinner skin than the limes that are commonly available in supermarkets. It also has a more tart flavor. Look for bottled Key lime juice alongside the bottled lemon juice in the supermarket. Feel free to substitute lemon juice, but the flavor won't be as tart.

Mini-Cinnis

20 rolls

prep: 7 minutes   cook: 12 minutes

1   (8-ounce) can refrigerated reduced-
      fat crescent dinner roll dough
4   teaspoons cinnamon sugar

Nonstick cooking spray

½   cup confectioners' sugar
2   teaspoons 1% low-fat milk

1 Preheat the oven to 375°. Unroll crescent dough, and cut dough crosswise with a sharp knife, forming 2 portions. Press perforations together with fingers. Sprinkle each portion of dough with 2 teaspoons cinnamon sugar.

2 Roll up 1 portion of dough, starting at long side and pressing firmly to eliminate air pockets; pinch seam to seal. Cut roll into 10 slices. Place slices cut-sides down on a baking sheet coated with nonstick cooking spray. Repeat with remaining dough portion.

3 Bake at 375° for 10 to 12 minutes or until rolls are golden.

4 Combine confectioners' sugar and milk in a small bowl, stirring with a whisk until smooth; drizzle over warm rolls with a small whisk.

Per roll: CALORIES 51 (34% from fat); FAT 1.9g (sat 0.8g); PROTEIN 0.8g; CARBOHYDRATE 8.5g; FIBER 0.1g; CHOLESTEROL 0mg; IRON 0.4mg; SODIUM 89mg; CALCIUM 3mg

Make Ahead

You can freeze unglazed cinnamon rolls in an airtight container for up to 1 month. When you're ready to serve 'em, just defrost in the microwave and drizzle with the fresh glaze.

Cheddar Drop Biscuits

1 dozen

prep: 6 minutes   cook: 8 minutes

2   cups low-fat biscuit baking mix
½   cup (2 ounces) shredded reduced-fat
        sharp Cheddar cheese
¾   cup fat-free milk

Nonstick cooking spray

2   tablespoons light stick butter, melted
½   teaspoon dried parsley, crushed
¼   teaspoon garlic powder

1 Preheat the oven to 450°. Combine baking mix and cheese; make a well in center of mixture. Add milk, stirring just until moist.

2 Drop dough by rounded tablespoonfuls 2" apart onto a baking sheet coated with nonstick cooking spray. Bake at 450° for 8 minutes or until golden.

3 Combine butter, parsley, and garlic powder; brush over warm biscuits.

Per biscuit: CALORIES 101 (32% from fat); FAT 3.6g (sat 1.4g); PROTEIN 3.3g; CARBOHYDRATE 14.6g; FIBER 0.3g; CHOLESTEROL 6mg; IRON 0.8mg; SODIUM 273mg; CALCIUM 163mg

Drop vs. Roll

Due to the higher proportion of liquid to the dry ingredients, drop biscuits have a thick batter instead of a soft dough like that of rolled biscuits—which is why they're dropped instead of kneaded and rolled. And because they're dropped, these biscuits take a lot less time to prepare than the rolled variety.

Rosemary Flatbread

10 servings

prep: 6 minutes   cook: 12 minutes

1   (13.8-ounce) can refrigerated pizza
        crust dough
Olive oil–flavored nonstick cooking spray

¼   cup chopped fresh rosemary or
        ¼ cup dried rosemary
2   tablespoons oil-packed sun-dried
        tomatoes, drained and chopped
1   clove garlic, minced
1   tablespoon grated fresh Parmesan
        cheese

1 Preheat the oven to 400°. Press
dough onto a baking sheet coated
with nonstick cooking spray.

2 Combine rosemary and remaining
3 ingredients in a small bowl. Coat
dough lightly with cooking spray, and
sprinkle rosemary mixture evenly over
dough.

3 Bake at 400° for 12 minutes or until
lightly browned. Cut into 10 equal
pieces.

*Per serving: CALORIES 104 (15% from fat); FAT 1.7g (sat 0.4g);
PROTEIN 3.3g; CARBOHYDRATE 19.3g; FIBER 0.2g;
CHOLESTEROL 0mg; IRON 1.2mg; SODIUM 295mg;
CALCIUM 10mg*

"*Shhh, this herb-flavored bread starts with pizza dough—
and it's ready in less than 20 minutes. Serve it alongside one
of my simmering soups that start on page 140.***"**

Roasted Red Pepper Crostini

20 servings

prep: 9 minutes   cook: 5 minutes

20 (¼"-thick) slices diagonally cut
     French bread baguette
Nonstick cooking spray
3   tablespoons chopped fresh basil,
     divided

1   (4¼-ounce) can chopped ripe olives,
     drained
¼   cup (1 ounce) crumbled feta cheese
     with basil and sun-dried tomato
1   (15-ounce) bottle roasted red bell
     peppers, drained and finely
     chopped

1 Preheat the oven to 400°. Place bread slices on a baking sheet; coat bread with nonstick cooking spray, and sprinkle evenly with 1½ tablespoons basil.

2 Bake at 400° for 5 minutes or until lightly toasted. Remove bread slices from pan to a wire rack; cool completely.

3 While bread cools, combine chopped olives and remaining 1½ tablespoons basil in a small bowl; stir in feta cheese and bell peppers.

4 Spoon 2 tablespoons olive mixture onto each bread slice.

Per crostini: CALORIES 48 (21% from fat); FAT 1.1g (sat 0.4g); PROTEIN 1.6g; CARBOHYDRATE 8g; FIBER 0.5g; CHOLESTEROL 1mg; IRON 0.5mg; SODIUM 156mg; CALCIUM 18mg

It's Italian!

Crostini is the Italian term for thin slices of toasted bread with savory toppings. These high-flavored ingredients make this appetizer a hands-down favorite.

BBQ Beans

4 servings

prep: 3 minutes   cook: 13 minutes

1   (15-ounce) can no-salt-added kidney
     or pinto beans, drained
3   tablespoons brown sugar
2   tablespoons dried onion flakes
¼   cup barbecue sauce

1 Combine all ingredients in a saucepan. Bring to a boil; cover, reduce heat to low, and simmer 5 minutes, stirring occasionally. Uncover and cook 5 more minutes.

Per ¾-cup serving: CALORIES 128 (4% from fat); FAT 0.6g (sat 0.1g); PROTEIN 6.3g; CARBOHYDRATE 25.1g; FIBER 2.6g; CHOLESTEROL 0mg; IRON 1.1mg; SODIUM 148mg; CALCIUM 33mg

"One taste of these baked beans, and you'll think they've simmered all day long. But just between you and me—they're done in just 13 minutes!**"**

Garlicky-Cheesy Smashed Potatoes

4 servings

prep: 5 minutes   cook: 6 minutes

1	pound Yukon gold potatoes
¼	cup light garlic-and-herbs spreadable cheese
½	cup fat-free milk
¼	teaspoon salt
¼	teaspoon pepper

1 Scrub potatoes; prick several times with a small fork or knife. Place on a microwave-safe platter. Microwave at HIGH 6 minutes or until tender.

2 Mash potatoes with a potato masher. Add cheese and remaining ingredients; mash to desired consistency.

Per ½-cup serving: CALORIES 117 (17% from fat); FAT 2.2g (sat 1.3g); PROTEIN 4.1g; CARBOHYDRATE 20.6g; FIBER 2.8g; CHOLESTEROL 8mg; IRON 0.7mg; SODIUM 203mg; CALCIUM 65mg

❝ *Thanks to the garlic cheese and Yukon golds, these mashed potatoes are a smashing big hit with my crew! And they're ready in record time—11 minutes!* **❞**

Curried Baked Pineapple

8 servings

prep: 5 minutes   cook: 10 minutes

2   (20-ounce) cans pineapple chunks in
        juice, drained
15 reduced-fat round buttery crackers,
        crushed
¼   cup packed brown sugar
¼   cup (1 ounce) shredded reduced-fat
        sharp Cheddar cheese
½   teaspoon curry powder

Fat-free butter spray

1 Preheat the oven to 450°. Place pineapple in an ungreased 7" x 11" baking dish. Combine cracker crumbs and
next 3 ingredients, stirring well. Sprinkle
cracker mixture over pineapple.

2 Coat cracker mixture with butter
spray (about 5 sprays). Bake at 450°
for 10 minutes or until lightly browned.

*Per ½-cup serving: CALORIES 119 (14% from fat); FAT 1.8g
(sat 0.5g); PROTEIN 1.7g; CARBOHYDRATE 25.2g; FIBER 1.2g;
CHOLESTEROL 3mg; IRON 0.7mg; SODIUM 89mg;
CALCIUM 79mg*

"*This dish is both savory and sweet, so I can never
decide whether to serve it as a side accompaniment
or as a dessert. I'll let you decide!***"**

Creamy Guacamole

2½ cups

prep: 9 minutes

1½ cups cubed peeled avocado (about
      2 avocados)
1   cup fat-free ricotta cheese (see tip)
⅓   cup coarsely chopped onion
2   tablespoons coarsely chopped fresh
      cilantro
2   tablespoons lime juice
1   tablespoon coarsely chopped seeded
      jalapeño pepper
½   teaspoon salt

1 Process all ingredients in a food processor until smooth, scraping sides of bowl once. Serve immediately.

Per tablespoon: CALORIES 15 (48% from fat); FAT 0.8g (sat 0.1g); PROTEIN 0.6g; CARBOHYDRATE 1.2g; FIBER 0.4g; CHOLESTEROL 1mg; IRON 0mg; SODIUM 36mg; CALCIUM 11mg

More, please!

This Mexican favorite features fat-free ricotta cheese, which not only makes the dip creamy, but also decreases the fat content since you don't need to use as much avocado. Serve with baked or light tortilla chips.

Creamy Crab Dip

1½ cups

prep: 7 minutes

½ cup plain low-fat yogurt
⅓ cup light mayonnaise
1 tablespoon minced fresh parsley or
    1 teaspoon dried parsley
1 tablespoon grated onion
2 teaspoons lemon juice
1 teaspoon Dijon mustard
¼ teaspoon dried dillweed
1 (8-ounce) container pasteurized fresh
    crabmeat, drained (see tip)

1 Combine first 7 ingredients in a small bowl; mix well. Stir in crabmeat.

2 Transfer mixture to a serving bowl. Cover and chill until ready to serve. Serve with Melba toast rounds or raw vegetables.

Per tablespoon: CALORIES 22 (53% from fat); FAT 1.3g (sat 0.3g); PROTEIN 1.8g; CARBOHYDRATE 0.7g; FIBER 0g; CHOLESTEROL 8mg; IRON 0.1mg; SODIUM 59mg; CALCIUM 17mg

Pasteurized Crabmeat

You can find containers of pasteurized crabmeat in the seafood department of your supermarket. It's a convenient alternative to fresh lump crabmeat, and it's practically shell free. Pasteurized crabmeat can be kept, unopened, for up to 30 days after the purchase date; use an open container within 4 days.

Baked Spinach-and-Artichoke Dip

(pictured on facing page)

2¾ cups

prep: 8 minutes   cook: 22 minutes

2	(6-ounce) packages fresh baby spinach
1	tablespoon butter
1	(8-ounce) package ⅓-less-fat cream cheese
1	clove garlic, chopped
1	(14-ounce) can artichoke hearts, drained and chopped
½	cup light sour cream
½	cup (2 ounces) shredded part-skim mozzarella cheese, divided

1 Microwave spinach in a large, microwave-safe bowl at HIGH 3 minutes or until wilted. Drain spinach well, pressing between paper towels. Chop spinach.

2 Preheat the oven to 350°. Melt butter in a nonstick skillet over medium-high heat. Add cream cheese and garlic; cook 3 to 4 minutes, stirring constantly, until cream cheese melts. Fold in spinach, artichokes, sour cream, and ¼ cup mozzarella cheese; stir until cheese melts.

3 Transfer mixture to a 1-quart shallow baking dish. Sprinkle with remaining ¼ cup mozzarella cheese.

4 Bake at 350° for 15 minutes or until hot and bubbly. Serve immediately with fresh pita wedges or baked pita chips.

❝*Check out my lightened version of a classic appetizer. Bet you can't tell the difference!***❞**

Per ¼-cup serving (not including dippers): CALORIES 113 (53% from fat); FAT 7g (sat 4.7g); PROTEIN 5.5g; CARBOHYDRATE 8.5g; FIBER 2.4g; CHOLESTEROL 24mg; IRON 1mg; SODIUM 340mg; CALCIUM 1mg

Shrimp Fried Rice,
page 20

Banana Pancakes with Golden
Banana Syrup, page 86

Buenos Burritos

(pictured on facing page)

4 servings

prep: 5 minutes   cook: 10 minutes

Nonstick cooking spray
½   pound chicken breast tenders
1   cup diced red bell pepper
½   cup salsa, divided

1   cup canned fat-free refried beans

4   (8") fat-free flour tortillas
Toppings: salsa, sour cream, Fiesta
      Corn Salad (page 110)

1 Coat a large nonstick skillet with nonstick cooking spray; place over medium-high heat until hot. Add chicken and pepper; sauté 3 minutes. Add ¼ cup salsa; reduce heat to medium-low, and cook mixture 2 minutes, stirring occasionally.

2 While chicken cooks, combine refried beans and remaining ¼ cup salsa in a small microwave-safe bowl. Cover with heavy-duty plastic wrap, and vent. Microwave at HIGH 2 minutes or until thoroughly heated, stirring after 1 minute.

3 Wrap tortillas in heavy-duty plastic wrap. Microwave at HIGH 30 to 45 seconds or until warm. Spread bean mixture evenly down centers of tortillas; top evenly with chicken mixture. Roll up tortillas. Serve with desired toppings.

Per serving: CALORIES 242 (4% from fat); FAT 1.1g (sat 0.2g); PROTEIN 19.8g; CARBOHYDRATE 37g; FIBER 5.1g; CHOLESTEROL 33mg; IRON 2.9mg; SODIUM 759mg; CALCIUM 39mg

❝*The fiber and protein in these burritos will keep your hunger satisfied for hours. Serve with Fiesta Corn Salad on page 110 to round out this festive meal.*❞

Fiesta Corn Salad

(pictured on page 108)

4 servings

prep: 5 minutes

2	cups frozen corn, thawed
½	cup salsa
1	scallion, sliced
3	tablespoons chopped radish
4	large romaine lettuce leaves

1 Combine first 4 ingredients in a medium bowl. Spoon mixture evenly over lettuce leaves.

Per serving: CALORIES 80 (6% from fat); FAT 0.5g (sat 0.1g); PROTEIN 3.0g; CARBOHYDRATE 19.1g; FIBER 2.8g; CHOLESTEROL 0mg; IRON 0.8mg; SODIUM 149mg; CALCIUM 18mg

"*Burritos and tacos come alive when you top 'em with this salsalike salad. Try it with the Buenos Burritos on page 109. The combo is muy bien!***"**

Mediterranean Chicken Couscous

8 servings

prep: 15 minutes   cook: 5 minutes

1¼ cups low-sodium fat-free chicken
       broth
1   (5.6-ounce) package toasted pine nut
       couscous mix

3   cups chopped cooked chicken
       (about 1 rotisserie chicken)
¼   cup chopped fresh basil or
       4 teaspoons dried basil
1   (4-ounce) package crumbled feta
       cheese
1   pint grape tomatoes, halved
1½ tablespoons fresh lemon juice
1   teaspoon grated lemon rind
¼   teaspoon pepper

1 Heat broth and seasoning packet
from couscous in a microwave-safe
bowl in the microwave at HIGH for 3 to
5 minutes or until broth begins to boil.
Place couscous in a large bowl, and stir
in broth mixture. Cover and let stand 5
minutes.

2 Fluff couscous with a fork; stir in
chicken and remaining 6 ingredients.
Serve warm or cold.

*Per 1-cup serving: CALORIES 212 (29% from fat); FAT 6.8g
(sat 3.1g); PROTEIN 21.3g; CARBOHYDRATE 16.9g; FIBER 1.4g;
CHOLESTEROL 58mg; IRON 1.2mg; SODIUM 455mg;
CALCIUM 89mg*

❝*No pots and pans needed here. Just use a glass
measuring cup to heat the broth and seasoning packet
in the microwave. Then place the dry couscous in a
serving bowl, and add the broth mixture. Once the remaining
ingredients are stirred in, dinner is served!*❞

Foolproof Pot Roast

4 servings

prep: 2 minutes   cook: 16 minutes

1   (16-ounce) package fully cooked beef
       pot roast in gravy

Nonstick cooking spray
1   large onion, thinly sliced

1   tablespoon light stick butter
½   teaspoon sugar
1   teaspoon balsamic vinegar
¼   teaspoon salt
¼   teaspoon pepper

1 Heat roast according to package directions. Remove roast from package, reserving liquid. Let stand 2 minutes. Cut into 8 pieces.

2 Coat a large nonstick skillet with nonstick cooking spray; place over medium-high heat until hot. Add onion, and sauté 10 minutes or until browned.

3 Add reserved liquid, roast, butter, and remaining ingredients to pan. Stir well, and bring to a boil. Boil 30 seconds or until thoroughly heated.

Per serving (2 pieces roast and 2 tablespoons sauce): CALORIES 181 (41% from fat); FAT 8.3g (sat 3.6g); PROTEIN 19.3g; CARBOHYDRATE 8.2g; FIBER 0.8g; CHOLESTEROL 56mg; IRON 1.6mg; SODIUM 756mg; CALCIUM 31mg

" *Talk about convenience! This savory main dish starts with a fully cooked pot roast (found in most supermarkets) and is doctored with just a few basic ingredients. And it's ready in less than 20 minutes—my idea of home-cooked goodness!* **"**

Spicy Grouper Fillets

4 servings

prep: 3 minutes   cook: 18 minutes

3	tablespoons all-purpose flour
½	teaspoon ground red pepper
¼	teaspoon salt
4	(6-ounce) grouper fillets (1" thick)
1	teaspoon olive oil
1	clove garlic, crushed

Lemon wedges (optional)

1 Combine first 3 ingredients in a large resealable plastic bag. Add fish; turn gently to coat.

2 Heat olive oil in a large nonstick skillet over medium heat. Add crushed garlic, and sauté 30 seconds; discard garlic. Add fish; cook 8 to 9 minutes on each side or until fish flakes easily with a fork. Serve with lemon wedges, if desired.

Per serving: CALORIES 190 (14% from fat); FAT 3g (sat 0.6g); PROTEIN 33.7g; CARBOHYDRATE 4.9g; FIBER 0.2g; CHOLESTEROL 63mg; IRON 1.8mg; SODIUM 238mg; CALCIUM 49mg

"This mild fish gets a punch of flavor from ground red pepper and garlic-infused olive oil."

Shrimp Scampi

4 servings

prep: 3 minutes   cook: 7 minutes

1½ tablespoons olive oil
1½ tablespoons prepared minced garlic

1½ pounds peeled and deveined jumbo
      shrimp (see note)

¼   cup finely chopped fresh flat-leaf
      parsley or 2 teaspoons dried
      parsley
1½ tablespoons lemon juice
½   teaspoon salt
⅛   teaspoon ground red pepper

1 Heat oil in a large nonstick skillet over medium-high heat; add garlic, and cook 1 minute.

2 Add shrimp to skillet, and cook 5 minutes or until shrimp are done, stirring occasionally.

3 Remove skillet from heat; stir in parsley and remaining ingredients.

Note: You'll need to start with 2¼ pounds of unpeeled jumbo shrimp if you'd rather peel and devein it yourself.

Per serving: CALORIES 245 (32% from fat); FAT 8.6g (sat 1.3g); PROTEIN 34.7g; CARBOHYDRATE 3.4g; FIBER 0.2g; CHOLESTEROL 259mg; IRON 4.4mg; SODIUM 549mg; CALCIUM 94mg

"*Serve this dish with French bread or a ½-cup portion of warm angel hair pasta. It's a winner either way.***"**

Everyday Entrées

"These high-flavored, quick-cooking dinnertime favorites are guaranteed to get you in and out of the kitchen fast so you can spend more time with your gang.**"**

Linguine Alfredo

6 servings

prep: 20 minutes   cook: 8 minutes

½   (16-ounce) box linguine

⅓   cup butter
2   cloves garlic, pressed
2   cups whipping cream
1   cup chicken broth, divided
¼   cup finely chopped fresh basil or
     1 tablespoon dried basil

1¼ cups grated Parmesan cheese
Freshly ground black pepper to taste

1 Cook pasta according to package directions; drain and keep warm.

2 Meanwhile, melt butter in a large skillet over medium heat. Add garlic, and sauté 2 minutes or until lightly browned. Stir in cream, ½ cup broth, and the basil. Increase heat to high, and bring to a boil; remove from heat.

3 Add pasta and remaining ½ cup broth. Sprinkle with Parmesan cheese, and toss to coat. Stir in pepper.

Pasta Pro

Pasta needs plenty of water to bubble around in as it cooks; use a 4- to 6-quart stock pot or Dutch oven, and use the package directions as a guide. Pasta should be cooked just until it's firm but tender. Overcooked pasta has a mushy texture.

Speedy Black Beans 'n' Mexican Rice

2 servings

prep: 5 minutes   cook: 3 minutes

1   (8.8-ounce) pouch ready-to-serve
     Mexican rice

1   (15-ounce) can black beans, rinsed
     and drained
1   (4.5-ounce) can chopped green
     chilies
2   tablespoons chopped fresh cilantro
Toppings: sour cream, salsa, diced
     tomato, shredded Cheddar cheese

1 Cook rice according to package directions.

2 Combine black beans and green chilies in a microwave-safe bowl. Microwave at HIGH 90 seconds. Stir in rice and cilantro. Serve immediately with desired toppings.

Mexican Beef 'n' Rice

Beef up this dish by substituting a pound of cooked lean ground beef for the black beans and 1 cup salsa for the green chilies. Prepare the recipe as directed, omitting the toppings. Serve with corn chips or in lettuce leaves, if desired. This recipe will make 4 servings.

Veggie-Salmon Packets

4 servings

prep: 6 minutes   cook: 18 minutes

Nonstick cooking spray
12   medium-sized fresh basil leaves

2   cups frozen whole kernel corn,
          thawed
1   cup halved grape tomatoes
1   clove garlic, pressed
4   (6-ounce) skinless salmon fillets
¼   teaspoon salt
¼   teaspoon freshly ground black
          pepper

Chopped fresh basil
Lemon wedges

1 Preheat the oven to 450°. Coat 1 side of 4 (12" x 18") pieces of heavy-duty aluminum foil with nonstick cooking spray. Place 3 basil leaves in center of each foil sheet.

2 Combine corn, tomatoes, and garlic; spoon evenly over basil leaves. Place salmon over vegetables. Sprinkle salmon evenly with salt and pepper. Fold foil over fish and vegetables; crimp edges to seal. Place packets on a baking sheet.

3 Bake at 450° for 15 to 18 minutes or until fish flakes easily with a fork. Serve with chopped fresh basil and lemon wedges.

"*Making this dish is a great way to capture summer's best flavors in one easy entrée. And there's virtually no cleanup!***"**

Greek Snapper on the Grill

12 servings

prep: 15 minutes   cook: 15 minutes

12 (8-ounce) snapper or grouper fillets
¼   cup olive oil
1   tablespoon Greek seasoning
24 (¼"-thick) lemon slices

Tartar sauce (see tip)

1 Rub fish fillets with oil; sprinkle evenly with Greek seasoning. Top each fillet with 2 lemon slices.

2 Place a large piece of lightly greased heavy-duty aluminum foil over cold grill rack. Preheat the grill to medium-high heat (350° to 400°). Arrange fish on foil.

3 Grill fish, covered, 15 minutes or until it flakes easily with a fork. Serve with tartar sauce.

Homemade Tartar Sauce

When time is on your side, try making your own tartar sauce. Stir together 1 cup mayonnaise, 2 tablespoons dill pickle relish, 2 tablespoons drained capers, 2 tablespoons chopped fresh chives, 1 tablespoon Dijon mustard, 1 teaspoon dried tarragon, 2 teaspoons lemon juice, and ¼ teaspoon pepper. Cover and chill until ready to serve. This makes 1½ cups.

Cod Fillets with Tomato Relish

4 servings

prep: 7 minutes   cook: 10 minutes

4	(6-ounce) cod fillets (about 1" thick) (see tip)
½	teaspoon salt
¼	teaspoon freshly ground black pepper
1	cup halved grape tomatoes
¼	cup coarsely chopped fresh parsley or 1 tablespoon dried parsley
¼	cup thinly sliced scallions
¼	cup extra virgin olive oil
1	tablespoon capers in juice
1	teaspoon lemon juice

1 Preheat the broiler. Sprinkle fish evenly with salt and pepper. Place fish on lightly greased broiler rack. Broil 4" from heat 8 to 10 minutes or until fish flakes easily with a fork.

2 Meanwhile, combine tomatoes and remaining 5 ingredients. Spoon mixture evenly over broiled fish.

"*Pollock, haddock, and grouper are good alternatives to cod in this recipe, and you can also serve the relish with your other favorite fish dishes.***"**

Crispy Shrimp with Remoulade

4 servings

prep: 8 minutes   cook: 18 minutes

⅔   cup mayonnaise
⅓   cup Dijon mustard with horseradish
1   scallion, minced
1   tablespoon drained capers
½   teaspoon Worcestershire sauce

1½ cups panko (Japanese) bread crumbs
1   pound peeled and deveined
      uncooked large shrimp
      (1½ pounds unpeeled)
3   large egg whites, beaten

½   cup canola oil

1 Stir together first 5 ingredients in a small bowl to make remoulade sauce; set aside.

2 Place bread crumbs in a shallow dish. Dip shrimp in egg whites; dredge in panko.

3 Heat oil in a large nonstick skillet over medium-high heat. Cook shrimp in batches 3 minutes on each side or until golden. Serve with remoulade sauce.

"For a variation, serve up these crispy shrimp po'boy style! Just slather the remoulade on your favorite hoagies, and add shrimp and shredded lettuce. Remoulade is a tangy mayonnaise-based French sauce that's flavored with mustard and sometimes capers, as we do here.**"**

Mango Chutney-Glazed Chicken Skewers

(pictured on page 39)

4 to 5 servings

prep: 9 minutes   cook: 8 minutes

1½ teaspoons chili powder
¾ teaspoon salt
¼ teaspoon ground cumin
2 teaspoons vegetable oil
Nonstick cooking spray

4 (6-ounce) skinned and boned chicken
  breasts (see tip)

1 (9-ounce) bottle mango chutney
  (remove 3 tablespoons chutney for
  brushing over chicken, reserving
  remaining portion for serving with
  grilled chicken)

1 Combine first 4 ingredients in a small bowl; set aside. Spray cold grill rack with nonstick cooking spray. Preheat the grill to medium-high heat (350° to 400°).

2 Place chicken between 2 sheets of heavy-duty plastic wrap, and pound to ½" thickness, using a meat mallet or rolling pin. Cut each breast half lengthwise into 4 strips. Place chicken strips in a bowl; add chili powder mixture, and toss well to coat chicken.

3 Thread 1 chicken strip onto each of 16 (6") skewers (see tip); brush chicken evenly with 3 tablespoons chutney. Grill chicken, covered, 3 to 4 minutes on each side or until done. Serve with remaining chutney.

"*If you use wooden skewers, be sure to soak 'em for at least 30 minutes before threading the chicken. This prevents the skewer ends from burning. Feel free to substitute chicken cutlets for chicken breasts—you'll save on cooking and prep times since cutlets need no pounding.***"**

Chicken Cutlets with Tomato-Olive Tapenade

4 servings

prep: 8 minutes   cook: 6 minutes

1   cup diced seeded tomato
¼   cup prepared refrigerated olive
       tapenade (see note)
1   tablespoon chopped fresh basil
1   teaspoon balsamic vinegar
½   teaspoon freshly ground black
       pepper, divided

1   pound chicken cutlets (see tip)
¼   teaspoon salt
1   tablespoon olive oil
¼   cup crumbled feta cheese

1 Combine tomato, olive tapenade, basil, vinegar, and ¼ teaspoon pepper in a bowl; set aside.

2 Sprinkle chicken cutlets with salt and remaining ¼ teaspoon pepper. Heat oil in a large nonstick skillet over medium-high heat. Add chicken, and cook 3 minutes on each side or until done; transfer to a serving platter. Spoon reserved tomato mixture over chicken, and sprinkle with cheese.

Note: You can find olive tapenade in the deli section of your supermarket.

Substitution Savvy

If you can't find chicken cutlets at your supermarket, it's okay to use boned and skinned chicken breasts. Place chicken breasts between 2 sheets of heavy-duty plastic wrap, and pound to ¼" thickness, using a meat mallet or rolling pin.

Asian Chicken Kabobs

4 servings

prep: 18 minutes   cook: 12 minutes

1½ pounds skinned and boned chicken
       breasts, cut into 1" cubes
¼ teaspoon salt
¼ teaspoon black pepper

1 medium-sized yellow bell pepper,
       seeded and cut into 1" pieces
1 medium-sized red bell pepper,
       seeded and cut into 1" pieces
1 (15-ounce) jar baby corn, drained

⅓ cup hoisin or teriyaki sauce
⅓ cup honey
1 clove garlic, pressed
½ teaspoon minced gingerroot or
       ⅛ teaspoon ground ginger

1 Preheat the grill to medium-high heat (350° to 400°). Sprinkle chicken evenly with salt and pepper.

2 Alternate chicken, pepper pieces, and corn on 8 (12") skewers. (See tip on page 122.)

3 Combine hoisin sauce and remaining 3 ingredients; brush on kabobs.

4 Grill, covered, 10 to 12 minutes, turning and basting with sauce mixture.

"*With these succulent kabobs, you get your meat and veggies in one easy step.***"**

Thai Chicken 'n' Rice Wraps

4 servings

prep: 9 minutes   cook: 3 minutes

4   teaspoons rice vinegar
2   tablespoons plus 2 teaspoons Asian
         chili sauce with garlic
2   tablespoons dark sesame oil, divided
¼   teaspoon ground ginger or
         1 tablespoon jarred minced ginger

2   cups shredded roasted chicken
1   large clove garlic, pressed
1   cup fresh cilantro leaves, chopped

8   leaves Boston or Bibb lettuce
2   cups warm cooked rice (see tip)

1 Combine vinegar, chili sauce, 1 table-spoon sesame oil, and the ginger in a small bowl; set aside.

2 Heat remaining 1 tablespoon sesame oil in a large skillet over medium heat. Add chicken and garlic; cook 2 minutes or until thoroughly heated. Stir in cilantro.

3 Place 2 lettuce leaves on each serving plate. Spoon rice evenly onto lettuce leaves; top with chicken mixture, and roll up. Serve wraps with reserved sauce.

Presto Rice

Don't have leftover rice? No worries! Now cooked rice comes in a convenient microwavable pouch, and it's ready in just 90 seconds! You can find it in an 8.8-ounce pack-age near the other rice in the supermarket.

Caprese-Style Chicken Pasta

4 servings

prep: 10 minutes   cook: 11 minutes

8	ounces rotini
1½	cups diced cooked chicken
2	cups grape tomatoes, halved
4	ounces fresh mozzarella cheese, cubed (about ¾ cup) (see tip)
⅓	cup grated Parmesan cheese
¼	cup Parmesan and roasted garlic dressing
½	cup torn fresh basil

1 Cook pasta according to package directions. Drain and place pasta in a large bowl.

2 Add chicken and remaining ingredients to warm pasta, and toss well. Serve immediately.

What's Caprese?

Caprese refers to a simple Italian salad containing basil, fresh mozzarella cheese, and tomato. Interestingly, it reproduces the colors of the Italian flag—green, white, and red. Fresh mozzarella is more delicately flavored, moist, and softer than regular mozzarella cheese. Look for it in the deli section of most supermarkets.

Skillet Chili Mac

4 servings

prep: 5 minutes   cook: 25 minutes

1   pound sweet Italian turkey sausage

1   tablespoon vegetable oil
1½   teaspoons chili powder
2   cups low-sodium chicken broth
¼   cup tomato paste

1   (12-ounce) package macaroni shells
     and cheese

1¾ cups salsa
Toppings: sour cream, chopped tomato,
     chopped fresh cilantro

1 Remove and discard casings from sausage.

2 Heat oil in a large skillet over medium-high heat; add sausage, stirring until sausage crumbles and is no longer pink. Drain well, and return to skillet. Add chili powder, stirring to coat sausage. Add chicken broth and tomato paste, stirring to loosen particles from bottom of skillet.

3 Stir in shell macaroni; bring to a boil. Reduce heat to medium-low; cover and simmer 8 minutes or until shells are tender, stirring occasionally.

4 Stir in cheese sauce from packet and the salsa; simmer, uncovered, 5 minutes or until thoroughly heated. Serve immediately with desired toppings.

"The gang will be all smiles when you serve up this enhanced version of mac and cheese. It's easy to keep the ingredients on hand for a quick dinner any night of the week."

Grilled Steak with Pineapple Salsa

4 servings

prep: 4 minutes   cook: 9 minutes

Nonstick cooking spray

1   (8-ounce) can pineapple slices, drained
2   tablespoons brown sugar
½   teaspoon kosher salt, divided
1   (1-pound) flat iron steak (see tip)
2   scallions

½   cup chunky salsa

1 Spray cold grill rack with nonstick cooking spray. Preheat the grill to medium-high heat (350° to 400°).

2 Sprinkle pineapple with brown sugar and ¼ teaspoon salt. Sprinkle steak with remaining ¼ teaspoon salt. Grill steak, pineapple, and scallions, covered, 3 to 4 minutes on each side or until steak is desired degree of doneness and pineapple and scallions are tender.

3 Let steak stand 5 minutes; cut diagonally across grain into thin slices. Finely chop pineapple and scallions; place in a small bowl, and stir in salsa. Serve pineapple salsa with steak.

Flat Iron Steak

This cut comes from the shoulder blade and is a great choice for grilling. If you can't find flat iron steak, flank steak is a good substitute. By allowing the steak to stand before slicing, the juices are preserved and it's easy to slice. Diagonally slicing the meat across the grain ensures extra tenderness.

Szechuan Beef with Broccoli

4 servings

prep: 9 minutes   cook: 15 minutes

1½ pounds boneless top sirloin steak
4   teaspoons canola oil, divided

1   teaspoon dark sesame oil
4   cups fresh broccoli florets
2   cloves garlic, minced

2   teaspoons cornstarch
⅓   cup Szechuan stir-fry and marinade
½   cup plus 2 tablespoons beef broth
½   cup coarsely chopped dry roasted
       peanuts
Warm cooked rice
Additional coarsely chopped dry roasted
    peanuts (optional)

1 Slice steak diagonally across the grain into very thin slices. Heat 2 teaspoons canola oil in a large nonstick skillet over medium-high heat. Add steak, and cook, stirring constantly, 5 minutes. Remove from skillet, and set aside.

2 Heat remaining 2 teaspoons canola oil and the sesame oil in skillet over medium-high heat; add broccoli, and cook 3 minutes. Add garlic; cook 30 seconds.

3 Combine cornstarch, Szechuan marinade, and beef broth, stirring until smooth. Add cornstarch mixture and steak to skillet; cook, stirring constantly, 2 minutes. Remove from heat, and stir in ½ cup peanuts. Serve over rice. Sprinkle with additional peanuts, if desired.

Chinese Cuisine

Szechuan refers to a style of Asian cooking indigenous to the Western region of China. It's characterized by hot and spicy dishes.

Grilled Roast Beef, Spinach, and Goat Cheese Pizza

4 to 6 servings

prep: 18 minutes   cook: 7 minutes

Nonstick cooking spray
1   (13.8-ounce) can refrigerated pizza
      crust
2   tablespoons olive oil, divided

6   ounces thinly sliced deli roast beef
2   cups loosely packed baby spinach
2   plum tomatoes, thinly sliced
4   ounces crumbled goat cheese
¼   teaspoon salt
Freshly ground pepper

1 Preheat the grill to medium-low heat (275° to 325°). Line a large baking sheet with heavy-duty aluminum foil; coat with nonstick cooking spray. Unroll dough on prepared foil. Starting at center, press out dough with hands to form a 9" x 13" rectangle. Brush dough with 1 tablespoon olive oil.

2 Invert dough onto grill rack; peel off foil. Grill, covered, 2 minutes or until bottom of dough is golden. Brush top with remaining 1 tablespoon olive oil; turn dough over, and grill, covered, 2 minutes or until bottom is set. Carefully remove crust from grill to aluminum foil-lined baking sheet.

3 Arrange roast beef, spinach, tomato slices, and goat cheese on crust. Sprinkle with salt and pepper. Return pizza to grill rack (pizza should slide easily). Grill, covered, 3 minutes or until crust is done and pizza is thoroughly heated.

Flip It Over

I find that using 2 expandable spatulas makes it easier to flip the dough on the grill than using just a regular spatula. If you don't have them, a large baking sheet with no sides or long-handled grilling tongs and a spatula will work, too.

Super Simple Sloppy Joes

8 servings

prep: 10 minutes   cook: 20 minutes

1½   pounds lean ground beef

1   (14½-ounce) can diced tomatoes
1¼   cups ketchup
½   cup bottled barbecue sauce
1   tablespoon Worcestershire sauce
8   hamburger buns, toasted

1 Cook ground beef in a large skillet over medium-high heat, stirring until it crumbles and is no longer pink; drain well. Return cooked beef to skillet.

2 Stir in tomatoes and next 3 ingredients. Reduce heat to low, and simmer 15 minutes or until thickened. Serve mixture on toasted buns.

Punch It Up!

If more kick is what you're yearning for, add some chopped pickled jalapeños (and some liquid from the jar) to get those taste buds jumping. Start with 1 tablespoon of each to suit your tastes.

Beefy Ravioli

4 servings

prep: 10 minutes   cook: 15 minutes

1   (24-ounce) package frozen beef
       ravioli

2   tablespoons butter
1   (8-ounce) package sliced fresh
       mushrooms
3   scallions, chopped
2   cloves garlic, minced
1   teaspoon dried Italian seasoning

1   (10-ounce) can diced mild tomatoes
       and green chilies, drained
2   tablespoons chopped fresh basil or
       2 teaspoons dried basil
1   cup whipping cream
½   cup grated Parmesan cheese
½   teaspoon salt

1 Prepare ravioli in a large Dutch oven according to package directions; drain and keep warm.

2 Melt butter in Dutch oven over medium-high heat. Add mushrooms and next 3 ingredients; sauté over medium-high heat 6 minutes or until mushrooms are tender.

3 Stir in diced tomatoes and green chilies, basil, and cream; bring to a boil. Reduce heat, and simmer 5 minutes, stirring occasionally. Stir in Parmesan cheese; add salt. Stir in cooked ravioli, tossing to coat.

No need to rely on the canned stuff when this chef-quality ravioli is served up in less than 30 minutes.

Grilled Lamb Chops with Mint and Feta Pesto

3 servings

prep: 8 minutes   cook: 10 minutes

6   (4-ounce) lamb loin chops
¼   cup extra virgin olive oil, divided
½   teaspoon salt, divided
½   teaspoon freshly ground black
       pepper, divided

½   cup packed fresh flat leaf parsley
¼   cup packed fresh mint leaves
2   cloves garlic, sliced
½   cup feta cheese

1 Preheat the grill to medium heat (300° to 350°). Brush lamb chops with 1 tablespoon olive oil; sprinkle chops with ¼ teaspoon salt and ¼ teaspoon pepper. Set aside.

2 Make pesto by processing parsley, mint, garlic, remaining 3 tablespoons olive oil, and the remaining ¼ teaspoon salt and ¼ teaspoon pepper in a food processor until finely chopped. Transfer pesto to a small bowl, and stir in feta cheese; set aside.

3 Grill lamb, covered, 5 minutes on each side or to desired degree of doneness. Serve with pesto.

Simple grilled lamb chops are enhanced with flavors of the Mediterranean when served with this Mint and Feta Pesto. Dish out 2 chops per person when serving this succulent entrée.

Orange-Honey Lamb Shish Kabobs

4 servings

prep: 10 minutes   cook: 8 minutes

4½   tablespoons chili-garlic sauce
3   tablespoons orange juice
       concentrate, thawed
¼   cup plus 2 tablespoons honey
1¼   teaspoons ground cumin
½   teaspoon salt
1½   pounds lamb top sirloin or boneless
       leg of lamb, cut into 1½" pieces

1   large navel orange, quartered
2   scallions

Warm cooked couscous

1 Stir together first 5 ingredients in a 2-cup glass measuring cup. Place lamb in a large bowl. Pour ¼ cup marinade over lamb, and toss to coat. Set remaining marinade aside to serve with kabobs. Let lamb marinate at room temperature 5 minutes.

2 While lamb marinates, preheat the grill to medium-high heat (350° to 400°). Cut each orange quarter crosswise into 2 pieces. Cut each scallion into 4 (3") pieces.

3 Remove lamb from marinade, leaving marinade in bowl. Thread orange pieces, lamb, and scallion pieces evenly onto skewers. (See tip on page 122.) Brush skewers with marinade remaining in bowl. Grill, covered, 4 minutes; turn and grill 4 more minutes. Serve over couscous and with reserved marinade.

Orange You Glad You Know?

Naval oranges are large, contain no seeds, and have a sweet, flavorful meaty flesh. Their thick, bright orange rind makes them ideal for grilling, as in this recipe.

Chipotle-Cinnamon Pork Chops

(pictured on page 3)

4 servings

prep: 8 minutes   cook: 16 minutes

1   teaspoon chipotle chili powder
½   teaspoon ground cinnamon
½   teaspoon kosher salt
1   tablespoon plus 2 teaspoons olive
      oil, divided
4   (1"-thick) boneless center-cut loin
      pork chops

1½ cups finely chopped fresh
      pineapple
2   tablespoons chopped fresh mint
1   tablespoon lemon juice
2   teaspoons sugar
¼   teaspoon crushed red pepper

1 Combine chili powder, cinnamon, salt, and 2 teaspoons oil; stir to make a paste. Rub paste over pork chops; let stand while making salsa.

2 Combine pineapple and remaining 4 ingredients; toss well, and set aside.

3 Heat remaining 1 tablespoon oil in a large nonstick skillet over medium heat. Add chops, and cook 7 to 8 minutes on each side or until done. Serve chops with salsa.

"*This refreshing pineapple salsa tames the punch of the chipotle chili powder. The salsa is also a good accompaniment to grilled fish.***"**

Gremolata-Topped Pork Chops

4 servings

prep: 8 minutes   cook: 16 minutes

1	cup packed fresh cilantro
½	teaspoon salt, divided
1	large clove garlic
¼	cup extra virgin olive oil
1	tablespoon lemon juice
⅛	teaspoon crushed red pepper
4	(1"-thick) boneless pork chops
¼	teaspoon freshly ground black pepper
3	tablespoons vegetable oil

1 Make gremolata by processing cilantro, ¼ teaspoon salt, the garlic, and next 3 ingredients in a food processor until coarsely puréed; set aside.

2 Sprinkle pork chops with remaining ¼ teaspoon salt and the black pepper. Heat oil in a large nonstick skillet over medium-high heat. Add chops, and cook 7 to 8 minutes. Turn chops; spoon gremolata evenly over chops. Cook 7 to 8 more minutes or until desired degree of doneness.

Gremolata

This mixture is traditionally made with parsley and served with hearty meat dishes. Here, cilantro replaces parsley as a refreshing update. Try gremolata with vegetables, too.

Orange-Glazed Ham Steak

6 servings

prep: 10 minutes   cook: 12 minutes

1   (2½-pound) package fully cooked, bone-in (½"-thick) center-cut ham steak

1   cup orange juice
1   (8-ounce) can pineapple tidbits in juice
¼   cup golden raisins
1   tablespoon Dijon mustard
1   teaspoon cornstarch
1   tablespoon cold water

1 Rinse ham, and pat dry (see tip).

2 Cook ham in a lightly greased skillet over medium-high heat 3 to 4 minutes on each side or until thoroughly heated. Remove ham, reserving drippings in skillet.

3 Stir in orange juice, and cook 2 minutes, stirring to loosen particles from bottom of skillet. Stir in pineapple, raisins, and mustard. Stir together cornstarch and 1 tablespoon cold water; add to orange juice mixture. Bring to a boil; cook, stirring constantly, 1 minute. Serve sauce with ham.

"*I rinse the ham here to wash away the excess sodium that was packaged with it as a preservative.***"**

Ham 'n' Cheese Strombolis

4 servings

prep: 14 minutes   cook: 10 minutes

1   (11-ounce) can refrigerated pizza
        dough
Olive oil-flavored nonstick cooking spray

6   ounces diced ham (about 1¼ cups)
        (see tip)
1   cup baby spinach leaves
1½ cups (5 ounces) shredded aged
        Provolone Italian cheese blend
½   teaspoon dried thyme

Warm marinara sauce

1 Preheat the oven to 425°. Unroll pizza dough onto a baking sheet coated with nonstick cooking spray; pat into an 11" x 14" rectangle. Cut dough into 4 (5½" x 7") rectangles.

2 Sprinkle rectangles evenly with ham, spinach, cheese, and thyme. Roll up dough jellyroll fashion starting at the short side of each rectangle. Pinch seams to seal, but do not seal ends of rolls. Arrange rolls 4" apart on same baking sheet; coat tops with cooking spray.

3 Bake at 425° for 10 minutes or until golden. Serve with marinara sauce.

This is a great way to use up any of that leftover baked ham. But no worries if there are no leftovers. Diced ham is readily available prepackaged in the supermarket meat department.

Super Soups &
Sandwiches

These super selections of savory soups and sandwiches are a snap to whip up. They're the perfect solutions when you need something fast—and tasty. Serve 'em individually, or match up your favorite soup-and-sandwich combo for a satisfying meal. Either way… you choose!

Potato-Vegetable Chowder

8 cups

prep: 15 minutes   cook: 15 minutes

2	tablespoons vegetable oil
1	medium onion, chopped
3	tablespoons all-purpose flour
2	cups milk
1	(10¾-ounce) can chicken broth
1	(10-ounce) package frozen chopped broccoli, thawed
½	(32-ounce) package frozen Southern-style hash browns (4 cups)
1	(8¼-ounce) can sliced carrots, rinsed and drained
1	cup (4 ounces) shredded sharp Cheddar cheese
¾	teaspoon salt
½	teaspoon pepper

1 Heat oil in a Dutch oven over medium-high heat. Add onion, and sauté until tender. Add flour, and cook, whisking constantly, 1 minute. Whisk in 1 cup milk and the chicken broth until blended. Stir in remaining 1 cup milk, the broccoli, hash browns, and carrots; cook over medium heat 7 minutes.

2 Stir in 1 cup cheese, the salt, and pepper; cook 5 minutes.

❝❝*Embrace the use of convenience products! When combined with other tasty items, you'll have a winning recipe, such as this veggie chowder. Sprinkle some extra cheese on top of each serving for an extra-cheesy punch.*❞

So-Quick Seafood Chowder

8 cups

prep: 15 minutes   cook: 15 minutes

12 ounces fresh or frozen orange
roughy fillets, thawed

½ (24-ounce) package frozen hash
browns with onions and peppers
1 cup water

1 (12-ounce) can evaporated milk
1 (10¾-ounce) can cream of potato
soup, undiluted
¼ cup bacon bits
2 teaspoons chopped fresh dill or
¾ teaspoon dried dillweed
¼ teaspoon salt
¼ teaspoon pepper
1 (2-ounce) jar diced pimientos,
drained

1 Cut fish fillets into 1" pieces.

2 Bring hash browns and 1 cup water to a boil in a large saucepan; reduce heat to low, cover, and simmer 5 minutes or until tender.

3 Stir in evaporated milk and next 5 ingredients; return to a boil. Add fish and pimientos; cover, reduce heat to low, and simmer 3 to 5 minutes or until fish flakes easily with a fork. Serve immediately.

❝*This hearty chowder is chock-full of fish and potatoes—just what the doctor ordered for those cold, blustery days! I don't recommend freezing this chowder because of its creamy texture, so be sure to invite the gang over or enjoy it within a couple of days.*❞

Quick Bean Soup

10 cups

prep: 10 minutes   cook: 15 minutes

2   teaspoons vegetable oil
1   large onion, chopped
1   small green bell pepper, chopped

1   (16-ounce) can kidney beans, rinsed
     and drained
1   (15-ounce) can pinto beans, rinsed
     and drained
1   (15-ounce) can black beans, rinsed
     and drained
2   (14½-ounce) cans stewed tomatoes,
     undrained
1   (14½-ounce) can chicken broth
1   cup picante sauce
1   teaspoon ground cumin

1 Heat oil in a Dutch oven over medium-high heat. Add onion and bell pepper, and sauté until tender.

2 Add kidney beans and remaining ingredients; bring to a boil. Cover, reduce heat to low, and simmer 10 minutes.

"Where's the beef? It's not in this hearty soup. No one will miss the meat after feasting on this satisfying soup, which is loaded with protein from 3 varieties of beans."

Creamy Chicken-and-Wild Rice Soup

8½ cups

prep: 10 minutes   cook: 15 minutes

3	(6½-ounce) packages frozen creamed chicken
3	tablespoons butter
2	cloves garlic, minced
1	(6-ounce) package long-grain and wild rice mix, cooked
1	(4-ounce) can sliced mushrooms, drained
½	teaspoon coarsely ground black pepper
1½	cups milk
2	teaspoons chicken bouillon granules

1 Thaw creamed chicken in microwave at MEDIUM (50% power) 8 to 9 minutes.

2 Meanwhile, melt butter in a large Dutch oven over medium-high heat; add garlic, and sauté until tender.

3 Reduce heat to medium, and stir in creamed chicken, rice, mushrooms, and pepper. Gradually stir in milk, and cook until thoroughly heated. Stir in bouillon granules.

"Creamed chicken morphs into a velvety soup with additions of wild rice, mushrooms, and other savory flavors. This soup is a good option to serve up during the week for a quick, no-fuss supper.**"**

Roasted Chicken Noodle Soup

5 cups

prep: 10 minutes   cook: 20 minutes

Nonstick cooking spray
2   cups frozen cubed hash brown
       potatoes
1½ cups frozen chopped onion, bell
       pepper, and parsley seasoning
       blend

2   (14-ounce) cans chicken broth
2   ounces wide egg noodles, uncooked
       (about 1 cup)
¼   teaspoon salt
⅛   teaspoon dried thyme

1   cup diced roasted chicken breast
1   cup evaporated milk

1 Coat a large saucepan with nonstick cooking spray; place over medium-high heat until hot. Add hash brown potatoes and seasoning blend; cook, stirring constantly, 3 minutes.

2 Add broth and next 3 ingredients; bring to a boil. Reduce heat to low, and simmer, partially covered, 7 minutes.

3 Add chicken and milk; cook 5 minutes or until noodles are tender.

"_Turn to this recipe when you have leftover roasted chicken on hand—it only takes 1 cup. But don't worry if you don't have leftovers; a rotisserie chicken from the supermarket works just as well._**"**

Dressed-Up Tomato Soup

11 cups

prep: 5 minutes   cook: 10 minutes

1   (28-ounce) can Italian-seasoned
        diced tomatoes

1   (26-ounce) can tomato soup,
        undiluted
1   (32-ounce) container chicken broth
½   teaspoon freshly ground black
        pepper

1 Process seasoned tomatoes in a food processor 3 to 4 times or until finely diced.

2 Stir together diced tomatoes, tomato soup, and remaining ingredients in a Dutch oven. Cook over medium heat 10 minutes or until thoroughly heated, stirring occasionally. Serve with sour cream and chopped fresh parsley, if desired.

❝*Canned tomato soup gets dressed up, thanks to a few extra ingredients that are probably already on your shelf.*❞

Tortellini Soup

7 cups

prep: 5 minutes   cook: 10 minutes

2   (14½-ounce) cans chicken broth
1   (14½-ounce) can diced tomatoes,
       undrained
1   (16-ounce) can chickpeas, rinsed and
       drained
2   medium cloves garlic, pressed
1   teaspoon dried basil, crushed
1   (9-ounce) package refrigerated
       cheese tortellini, uncooked

2   tablespoons chopped fresh parsley
2   tablespoons grated Parmesan cheese

1 Bring first 5 ingredients to a boil in a large saucepan. Stir in tortellini, and return to a boil.

2 Reduce heat to low, and simmer 3 minutes. Stir in parsley, and sprinkle with Parmesan cheese. Serve immediately.

❝*Your bowls will be full of the flavors of Italy when you serve this pasta soup. If the gang's really hungry, include Italian bread or one of the savory sandwiches in this chapter.*❞

Chicken Gumbo

5 cups

prep: 3 minutes   cook: 16 minutes

1   teaspoon olive oil
1   (10-ounce) package frozen chopped
     onion, celery, and bell pepper
     seasoning blend
2   tablespoons all-purpose flour

1   cup canned chicken broth
¼   teaspoon hot sauce
1   (14½-ounce) can Cajun-style stewed
     tomatoes, undrained

1   (10-ounce) package frozen sliced
     okra
1½ cups frozen diced cooked chicken
     breast

1 Heat oil in a large nonstick skillet over medium-high heat. Add frozen seasoning blend, and cook, stirring constantly, 3 minutes. Add flour, stirring well.

2 Add chicken broth, hot sauce, and tomatoes; cook 3 minutes or until mixture is slightly thickened.

3 Add okra and chicken; cover and cook 8 minutes or until okra is tender.

❝Gumbo doesn't have to simmer all day to be good. This pot of goodness is ready in less than 20 minutes! French bread makes the perfect go-along.**❞**

Beefy Black Bean Chili

(pictured on page 174)

7 cups

prep: 2 minutes   cook: 15 minutes

1	pound ground round
2	(15-ounce) cans black beans, undrained
1	cup medium or hot chunky salsa
2	(8-ounce) cans tomato sauce
1	tablespoon chili seasoning mix

1 Cook beef in a large saucepan over medium-high heat, stirring until it crumbles and is no longer pink. Drain, if necessary.

2 While beef cooks, drain and mash 1 can of beans. Add mashed beans, undrained beans, salsa, tomato sauce, and seasoning mix to saucepan; stir well. Cook over medium heat 10 minutes or until thoroughly heated.

3 Spoon into servings bowls, and serve with sour cream, shredded Cheddar cheese, and chopped scallions, if desired.

"_Black beans and salsa give this chili a Mexican twist. Serve with corn or tortilla chips. ¡Olé!_**"**

Barbecue Chili

8 servings

prep: 5 minutes   cook: 20 minutes

1½ pounds shredded barbecue pork
      (see tip)
2   (14½-ounce) cans diced tomatoes
      with green pepper, celery, and
      onion
1   (8-ounce) can tomato sauce
1   cup barbecue sauce (see tip)
3   tablespoons chili powder

1 Stir together all ingredients in a Dutch oven; bring to a boil over medium-high heat, stirring occasionally. Cover, reduce heat to low, and simmer 15 minutes, stirring occasionally. If desired, serve with sour cream, shredded lettuce, shredded cheese, diced onion, and tortilla chips.

" *Pick up shredded pork from your favorite restaurant, or use one of the ready-to-serve products from your supermarket. You'll find that barbecue sauce can range in flavor from sweet to smoky, so choose whichever brand you prefer for this chili.* **"**

Bacon-Ranch Quesadillas

4 servings

prep: 15 minutes   cook: 8 minutes

Nonstick cooking spray

¼   cup Ranch dressing
4   (8") flour tortillas
1   cup (4 ounces) shredded Mexican
      four-cheese blend
4   bacon slices, cooked and crumbled
1   plum tomato, seeded and chopped

Ranch dressing
Salsa

1 Coat a large nonstick skillet with nonstick cooking spray. Place skillet over medium-high heat until hot.

2 Spread ¼ cup Ranch dressing evenly on 1 side of each tortilla. Place 1 tortilla dressing-side up in hot skillet; top evenly with half each of cheese, bacon, and tomato. Lightly press a second tortilla, dressing-side down, on top of mixture. Coat lightly with cooking spray, and cook 1 to 2 minutes on each side or until golden. Repeat procedure with remaining tortillas, cheese, bacon, and tomato.

3 Cut each quesadilla into wedges. Serve with Ranch dressing and salsa.

"Lasso in your young-uns with these tasty quesadillas, which are perfect as snacks or as mealtime sandwiches.**"**

Dusted Catfish Sandwiches

4 servings

prep: 10 minutes   cook: 8 minutes

1   cup mayonnaise
3   tablespoons orange juice
1   to 2 teaspoons minced canned
        chipotle chilies in adobo sauce
1½ teaspoons salt, divided

¼   cup self-rising cornmeal
2   teaspoons ground cumin
4   (6-ounce) catfish fillets (see tip)
Nonstick cooking spray

4   whole wheat sandwich buns, split
        and toasted
Tomato slices
Shredded lettuce

1 Preheat the grill to medium-high heat (350° to 400°). Stir together first 3 ingredients and ½ teaspoon salt. Set aside.

2 Combine cornmeal, cumin, and remaining 1 teaspoon salt. Rinse fish, and dredge in cornmeal mixture. Spray fish evenly with nonstick cooking spray.

3 Grill fish, covered, 3 to 4 minutes on each side or just until fish begins to flake with a fork.

4 Serve on buns with mayonnaise mixture, tomato slices, and shredded lettuce.

Have It Your Way

Instead of catfish, feel free to use other thin fillets of mild, firm-textured fish, such as cod, tilapia, perch, or orange roughy. Both fresh and frozen fish will work for these sandwiches.

Chicken-Slaw Wraps

4 servings

prep: 25 minutes

2   (6-ounce) packages fully cooked
       chicken breast strips, chopped
1½   cups shredded coleslaw mix with
       carrots (see note)
⅓   cup Ranch dressing
¼   cup sweet pickle relish

8   deli-style white Cheddar cheese slices
       (about 3 ounces)
4   sun-dried tomato basil wraps

1 Stir together first 4 ingredients in a large bowl.

2 Place 2 cheese slices in a single layer on 1 side of each wrap; top each evenly with about ¾ cup chicken mixture. Roll up jelly-roll fashion; wrap in plastic wrap, twisting ends of wrap to seal. Chill up to 8 hours, if desired. To serve, cut wraps in half.

Note: You can substitute 1½ cups shredded lettuce for the coleslaw mix.

" *You'll score big with the family with these handy wraps. They're just the thing for evenings-on-the-run or to pack in the lunch box.* **"**

Ham 'n' Turkey Rollups

6 to 12 servings

prep: 10 minutes

1 (8-ounce) container garlic-and-herb whipped cream cheese spread
½ cup chopped bottled roasted red bell peppers

6 (8") flour tortillas
3 cups firmly packed baby spinach leaves
12 ounces sliced lean deli ham
12 ounces sliced deli turkey breast

1 Stir together cream cheese and peppers in a small bowl until smooth.

2 Spread about ¼ cup cream cheese mixture evenly over 6 tortillas. Place ½ cup spinach on each tortilla. Top evenly with ham and turkey slices. Roll up jelly-roll fashion, and cut in half. Secure each half with a wooden toothpick.

"With this recipe, we sneak some greens into the gang's rollups—betcha they won't mind at all! For heartier appetites, these rollups will serve 6, or pair halves with a soup or salad to stretch 'em for 12 servings."

Warm Prosciutto-Stuffed Focaccia

6 servings

prep: 10 minutes   cook: 15 minutes

1   (9-ounce) round loaf focaccia bread
    (see tip)
3   ounces thinly sliced prosciutto
    (see tip)
4   ounces thinly sliced Muenster cheese
1   (6-ounce) package fresh baby
    spinach
¼   cup bottled roasted red bell peppers,
    drained
2   tablespoons light balsamic vinaigrette

1 Preheat the oven to 350°. Cut bread in half horizontally, using a serrated knife. Top bottom bread half with prosciutto and next 3 ingredients. Drizzle with balsamic vinaigrette; cover with top bread half. Wrap in aluminum foil; place on a baking sheet.

2 Bake at 350° for 15 minutes or until warm. Cut focaccia into six wedges. Serve immediately.

Switch It Up
Look for focaccia bread in your supermarket's bakery. If you can't find it, a round Italian loaf or ciabatta bread can be used instead. Also, 6 ounces of ham may be substituted for the prosciutto in this sandwich.

Giant Ham-and-Pepper Salad Sandwich

(pictured on page 2)

4 servings

prep: 15 minutes

1 (16-ounce) round Italian bread loaf
3 tablespoons honey mustard

2 scallions, chopped
1 (3-ounce) package cream cheese, softened
1 tablespoon mayonnaise
1 pound deli ham, thinly sliced
¼ cup pickled sliced banana peppers, drained
1 (6-ounce) package Swiss cheese slices
4 (1-ounce) American cheese slices
Tomato slices
Lettuce leaves

1 Cut off top ⅓ of bread loaf, and spread cut side of top with honey mustard; set aside.

2 Scoop out soft center of remaining bread, leaving a ¼"-thick shell. (Reserve soft center of loaf for other uses, if desired.)

3 Stir together scallions, cream cheese, and mayonnaise; spread in bottom of bread shell. Layer with ham and remaining 5 ingredients; cover with bread top, honey mustard-side down. Cut into 4 wedges to serve.

" *Bring your appetite when you sit down to feast on this giant sandwich!* **"**

Italian Club Sandwich

4 servings

prep: 25 minutes   cook: 6 minutes

12   (½"-thick) slices Italian bread
¼   cup Italian dressing
⅓   cup shredded Parmesan cheese

½   cup mayonnaise
½   cup mustard
½   pound thinly sliced Genoa salami
½   pound thinly sliced mortadella or
        bologna
4   (1-ounce) provolone cheese slices
Romaine lettuce leaves
3   plum tomatoes, sliced
8   bacon slices, cooked and cut in half

1 Preheat the oven to 375°. Arrange bread on a baking sheet. Brush slices evenly with Italian dressing, and sprinkle with Parmesan cheese. Bake at 375° for 5 minutes or until lightly toasted.

2 Spread untoasted sides of bread slices evenly with mayonnaise and mustard. Layer each of 4 bread slices mayonnaise-side up evenly with salami, mortadella, and provolone. Top with 4 more bread slices, mayonnaise-side up; layer each evenly with lettuce, tomatoes, and bacon. Top with remaining 4 bread slices, mayonnaise-side down. Secure with wooden toothpicks, and cut in half.

❝*Tired of the same ol' sandwich? Then join the club—the double-decker kind! This classic sandwich perks up the appetite and is given an Italian flair with sliced salami and mortadella.***❞**

Sloppy Joe Meatball Hoagies

4 servings

prep: 10 minutes   cook: 15 minutes

1   tablespoon vegetable oil
1   small sweet onion, diced
1   small green bell pepper, diced

1   (15.5-ounce) can Sloppy Joe sauce
30   to 32 frozen cooked meatballs
     (see tip)
4   hoagie buns, split and toasted

1 Heat oil in a large skillet over medium-high heat. Add onion and pepper, and sauté for 3 minutes.

2 Add sauce and meatballs to skillet; cook 10 minutes or until thoroughly heated, stirring often. Spoon evenly onto hoagie buns.

Meatballs in a Hurry

No need to mix and form your own meatballs! Look for the cooked and frozen variety in your supermarket. The package usually comes with 30 to 32 meatballs per pound.

Triple B Sandwiches

6 servings

prep: 10 minutes   cook: 5 minutes

½ (4-ounce) package crumbled blue
     cheese
¼ cup butter, softened

½ (8-ounce) package cream cheese
½ cup sour cream
1 tablespoon finely chopped onion
⅛ teaspoon garlic salt
1 (12-ounce) package bacon, cooked
     and crumbled

12 slices pumpernickel or sourdough
       bread, toasted
12 ounces thinly sliced cooked roast
       beef
1 tablespoon chopped fresh chives
2 tomatoes, thinly sliced
1 head green leaf lettuce, separated

1 Combine blue cheese and butter in a small bowl; set aside.

2 Combine cream cheese and next 3 ingredients in a small saucepan; cook over low heat, stirring constantly, until blended. Cool; stir in bacon.

3 Spread blue cheese mixture over half of bread slices; top evenly with roast beef. Spread cream cheese mixture on remaining bread slices, and sprinkle with chives. Serve open faced with tomato slices and lettuce leaves.

❝*Beef, bacon, and blue cheese make up these open-faced Triple B Sandwiches. They're a welcome change for lunch or dinner!*❞

Sassy Sides & Salads

"Look no further for that perfect go-along for dinner tonight. Here, you'll find a variety of sides, salads, and dressings that mix up in a hurry!"

Warm Cinnamon Apples

6 servings

prep: 10 minutes   cook: 10 minutes

4   McIntosh apples, peeled and sliced
       (about 2 pounds)
½   cup packed light brown sugar
1   teaspoon ground cinnamon
¼   teaspoon ground nutmeg

2   tablespoons water
1   tablespoon butter

1 Toss together first 4 ingredients in a large resealable plastic bag, tossing to coat apples.

2 Cook apple mixture, water, and butter in a medium saucepan over medium heat 8 to 10 minutes or until apples are tender, stirring occasionally.

Picking Apples
If you can't find McIntosh apples, substitute another baking apple, such as Rome or Gala; or try a crisp, tart green apple, such as Granny Smith.

Grilled Asparagus

4 servings

prep: 10 minutes   cook: 4 minutes

1   pound fresh asparagus

1   tablespoon olive oil
1   teaspoon balsamic vinegar
¼   teaspoon salt
¼   teaspoon pepper

1   teaspoon grated lemon rind

1 Preheat the grill to medium-high heat (350° to 400°). Snap off and discard tough ends of asparagus.

2 Combine olive oil, balsamic vinegar, salt, and pepper in a shallow dish or large resealable plastic bag; add asparagus, turning to coat.

3 Remove asparagus from oil mixture. Grill asparagus, covered, 2 to 4 minutes or until tender, turning once. Remove asparagus, and sprinkle evenly with grated lemon rind; serve immediately.

"The grilling time is for pencil-thin asparagus. For thicker asparagus, you'll need to increase the time."

Oh-So-Simple Green Beans Amandine

2 servings

prep: 5 minutes   cook: 10 minutes

½   pound green beans

1   tablespoon butter
2   tablespoons sliced almonds

Salt and pepper to taste

1 Cook beans in boiling salted water 5 minutes or until crisp-tender; drain.

2 Melt butter in a medium skillet over medium heat until hot; add almonds, and sauté 2 minutes or until golden.

3 Add beans to skillet; sauté 2 minutes. Sprinkle beans with salt and pepper to taste. Serve immediately.

"Impress someone special with a side of these simple beans. Amandine is the French term for a dish that's garnished with almonds. Your guests will squeal 'ooh la la' for these savory veggies!"

Quick Parmesan Couscous

4 servings

prep: 5 minutes   cook: 5 minutes

2   cups chicken broth
1   tablespoon butter
1   (10-ounce) package plain couscous, uncooked (see tip)

⅓   cup grated Parmesan cheese
1   tablespoon lemon juice
1   tablespoon olive oil
¼   teaspoon salt
⅛   teaspoon freshly ground black pepper

1 Bring chicken broth and butter to a boil in a large saucepan. Stir in couscous; cover and remove from heat. Let stand 5 minutes.

2 Stir in Parmesan cheese and remaining ingredients. Fluff couscous with a fork. Serve immediately.

Choose Couscous

Couscous is a tiny pasta made from coarsely ground semolina wheat. It makes a great alternative to rice—and cooks almost instantly. Look for it in the rice section of your supermarket.

Ranch Noodles

4 to 6 servings

prep: 5 minutes   cook: 10 minutes

1   (8-ounce) package egg noodles

¼   cup butter
½   cup sour cream
½   cup Ranch dressing
½   cup grated Parmesan cheese

1 Cook egg noodles according to package directions; drain and return to pot.

2 Stir in butter and remaining ingredients. Serve immediately.

Switch It Up for an Entrée
Substitute an 8-ounce package of thin spaghetti for the egg noodles, and add chopped cooked ham and steamed broccoli. Sauté the ham in a lightly greased skillet over medium-high heat to crisp it up and give it a smoky bacon-like flavor.

Bow Tie Pasta Toss

4 to 6 servings

prep: 3 minutes   cook: 12 minutes   stand: 10 minutes

8   ounces uncooked bow tie pasta
¾   teaspoon salt, divided

1   cup grape tomatoes, cut in half
1   (2.25-ounce) can sliced ripe black
       olives, drained
1   tablespoon finely chopped sweet
       onion

3   tablespoons olive oil
3   tablespoons balsamic vinegar
1   small clove garlic, pressed
1   teaspoon chopped fresh oregano or
       ¼ teaspoon dried oregano
½   (4-ounce) package crumbled feta
       cheese

1 Prepare pasta according to package directions, adding ½ teaspoon salt to water; drain well.

2 Place pasta in a large bowl, and stir in tomatoes, olives, and onion.

3 Whisk together olive oil, next 3 ingredients, and remaining ¼ teaspoon salt; add to pasta mixture, tossing to coat. Let stand 10 minutes; stir in feta.

Kitchen Express

Get in and out of the kitchen faster by substituting 6 tablespoons balsamic vinaigrette for the olive oil, vinegar, garlic, and oregano. Then proceed as directed in the recipe.

Gingered Sugar Snap Peas

5 servings

prep: 10 minutes   cook: 6 minutes

2	teaspoons olive oil
1	pound fresh sugar snap peas
2	cloves garlic, chopped
2	teaspoons grated fresh ginger (see tip)
1	teaspoon chopped walnuts, toasted
¾	teaspoon salt

1 Heat oil in a nonstick skillet over medium-high heat. Add peas, and cook 3 to 5 minutes or until crisp-tender, stirring occasionally.

2 Stir in garlic and remaining ingredients; cook 1 minute. Serve immediately.

Ginger Jar

Look for already minced cured ginger in the produce department of your supermarket. Or substitute about ⅛ teaspoon of ground ginger for the grated fresh ginger.

Basil Rice Pilaf

4 to 6 servings

prep: 5 minutes   cook: about 2½ minutes

2   (8.8-ounce) pouches microwaveable
      rice pilaf

2   tablespoons chopped fresh basil or
      2 teaspoons dried basil
2   teaspoons lemon juice
2   teaspoons olive oil

1 Microwave rice pilaf according to package directions; spoon rice into a serving bowl.

2 Stir in basil, lemon juice, and olive oil; serve immediately.

"Thanks to the availability these days of a variety of microwaveable products in the market, you can dish up a healthy serving of rice pilaf in less than 10 minutes!"

Citrusy Pecan Wild Rice

4 to 6 servings

prep: 10 minutes   cook: 10 minutes

1⅓ cups chicken broth
2   teaspoons butter
¼   teaspoon salt

1   (2.75-ounce) package quick-cooking
     wild rice

4   scallions, thinly sliced
½   cup golden raisins
⅓   cup chopped pecans, toasted
⅓   cup orange juice
¼   cup chopped fresh parsley or
     1 tablespoon dried parsley
1   tablespoon olive oil
¼   teaspoon salt
¼   teaspoon pepper

1 Bring first 3 ingredients to a boil in a medium saucepan.

2 Add rice; cover, reduce heat to low, and simmer 5 minutes or until rice is tender. Drain off excess liquid. Fluff with a fork.

3 Add scallions and remaining ingredients to rice; toss gently to combine.

Orange Zest

For a more pronounced citrus flavor, toss a teaspoon of grated orange rind (zest) into the rice. Just gently rub a clean orange against a fine grater or zester. Be careful to remove just the colored skin and not the white pith, which tends to be very bitter.

Seasoned Sweet Potato Fries

4 servings

prep: 10 minutes   cook: 12 minutes

1½ pounds sweet potatoes (about
        3 medium-size)
Nonstick cooking spray
½   teaspoon seasoned salt

1 Pierce sweet potatoes several times with a fork. Place on a microwave-safe plate; cover with damp paper towels. Microwave at HIGH 6 to 8 minutes or until tender. Let stand 5 minutes. Peel and cut potatoes in half lengthwise. Cut into (½" x 3") strips. Coat evenly with nonstick cooking spray, and sprinkle evenly with salt.

2 Coat cold grill rack with cooking spray. Preheat the grill to medium-high heat (350° to 400°). Grill potatoes, covered, 1 to 2 minutes on each side or until grill marks appear on fries.

Note: This recipe was tested in an 1100-watt microwave oven.

The next time the gang wants fries, serve up these tasty veggies. Sweet potatoes are full of nutrients, and this version is a healthier choice than the traditional fried variety.

Simple Stir-fry

4 to 6 servings

prep: 5 minutes   cook: 11 minutes

1   (14.5-ounce) can low-sodium fat-free
    chicken broth
¼   cup lite soy sauce
1   to 2 tablespoons chili-garlic sauce
2   tablespoons cornstarch
1   tablespoon brown sugar
1   teaspoon ground ginger

2   tablespoons dark sesame oil
1   (16-ounce) package frozen stir-fry
    vegetables

1 Whisk together first 6 ingredients in a medium bowl.

2 Heat sesame oil in a large skillet or wok over medium-high heat 2 minutes. Add vegetables, and stir-fry 5 to 7 minutes. Add broth mixture, and stir-fry 1 to 2 minutes or until sauce thickens and vegetables are tender.

One-Dish Terrific

Make this simple side into a hearty one-dish meal by stirring in 3 cups of chopped cooked chicken, pork, or beef.

Italian Salad

8 servings

prep: 15 minutes

1   head iceberg lettuce, torn (about
        1 pound)
1   (9-ounce) package frozen artichoke
        hearts, thawed (*see tip*)
1   (2.25-ounce) can sliced ripe black
        olives, drained
1   small red bell pepper, chopped
1¼ cups large-cut croutons
½   cup sliced peperoncini salad
        peppers
¼   cup chopped red onion

¾   cup refrigerated creamy Asiago-
        peppercorn or Parmesan-
        peppercorn dressing

1 Place lettuce in a 4-quart bowl.
    Arrange artichoke hearts and next
5 ingredients over lettuce.

2 Top with dressing; gently toss to com-
    bine. Serve immediately.

Itsa Easy!
No need to cook the frozen artichoke hearts—just thaw 'em,
and pat dry. Or you can substitute 1 (14-ounce) can artichoke
hearts, drained.

Summer Veggie Medley

(pictured on facing page)

6 to 8 servings

prep: 15 minutes   cook: 15 minutes

Nonstick cooking spray
6   large ears fresh corn, husks removed

3   cups lightly packed baby arugula
2   cups grape or cherry tomatoes
5   bacon slices, cooked and crumbled
¼   cup chopped fresh cilantro
¼   cup lime juice
2   cloves garlic, minced
Salt and freshly ground black pepper to
    taste

1 Coat cold grill rack with nonstick cooking spray. Preheat the grill to medium-high heat (350° to 400°). Coat corn with cooking spray. Grill corn, covered, 12 to 15 minutes or until lightly browned and done, turning occasionally. Remove corn from grill, and cool slightly.

2 Hold each grilled cob upright on a cutting board; carefully cut downward, cutting kernels from cob. Discard cobs.

3 Combine corn kernels, arugula, and next 5 ingredients, tossing to coat. Season to taste with salt and pepper. Serve immediately.

❝When corn is at its height of freshness, pull out this recipe to enjoy the bounty of the summer garden.**❞**

Beefy Black Bean Chili,
page 148

PB & Chocolate Pan Cookies,
page 186

Grilled Sweet Potato Salad

(pictured on facing page)

4 servings

prep: 10 minutes   cook: 12 minutes

4   sweet potatoes, peeled and cut into
        ½" slices
Nonstick cooking spray

½   cup diced red bell pepper
¼   cup sliced scallions
¼   cup chopped fresh flat-leaf parsley
        or 1 tablespoon dried parsley
Basil Vinaigrette

1 Preheat the grill to medium-high heat (350° to 400°). Coat both sides of sweet potato slices with nonstick cooking spray.

2 Grill potatoes, covered, 6 minutes on each side or until tender. Cool slightly, and cut into 1" cubes.

3 Combine potatoes, bell pepper, scallions, and parsley in a large bowl; toss with Basil Vinaigrette.

Basil Vinaigrette

¼   cup bottled light red wine vinegar-
        and-olive oil dressing
1   tablespoon chopped fresh basil or
        1 teaspoon dried basil
2   teaspoons balsamic vinegar

1 Whisk together all ingredients in a small bowl. Makes ¼ cup

❝Bottled dressing is enhanced here with chopped basil. You'll want to dress the potatoes while they're still warm so that they can absorb the tangy flavor.**❞**

Toasted Pecans-and-Avocado Salad

8 servings

prep: 15 minutes

1   head Bibb lettuce
2   avocados, peeled and thinly sliced
1   red bell pepper, thinly sliced
1   yellow bell pepper, thinly sliced
½   cup chopped toasted pecans
Tangy Dijon Dressing

1 Arrange lettuce leaves on a serving platter. Top evenly with avocado and bell pepper slices; sprinkle with pecans. Drizzle with desired amount of dressing.

Tangy Dijon Dressing

⅓   cup olive oil
2   tablespoons lemon juice
2   tablespoons water
1   tablespoon sugar
2   teaspoons Dijon mustard
⅛   teaspoon salt
⅛   teaspoon black pepper

1 Whisk together all ingredients in a small bowl. Store in an airtight container in the refrigerator up to 1 week. Makes about ⅔ cup

"*Get a jump on this recipe, and prepare the dressing ahead of time. It'll keep in the fridge up to 1 week.***"**

Grilled Romaine Salad

8 servings

prep: 10 minutes   cook: 11 minutes

4   romaine lettuce bunches
1   small red onion
2   tablespoons olive oil

Nonstick cooking spray

Buttermilk-Chive Dressing (see tip)
½   cup freshly shaved Parmesan cheese
Kosher salt and freshly ground pepper to
       taste

Buttermilk-Chive Dressing

Stir together 1¼ cups of refrigerated Ranch dressing with 2 tablespoons of chopped fresh chives. Store dressing in the refrigerator up to 3 days. Makes 1¼ cups.

1 Pull off tough outer leaves of romaine bunches, and discard; cut bunches in half lengthwise, keeping leaves intact. Peel onion, and cut in half vertically, keeping core (root end and top) intact. Cut each half into 4 wedges. Brush lettuce and onion evenly with olive oil.

2 Coat cold grill rack evenly with nonstick cooking spray. Preheat the grill to medium heat (300° to 350°). Grill onion wedges, covered, 3 to 4 minutes on each side or to desired degree of doneness. Remove onion wedges from grill.

3 Place romaine halves cut-sides down on grill. Grill, uncovered, 2 to 3 minutes or just until wilted.

4 Divide grilled lettuce cut-sides up evenly among serving plates. Top each with 1 onion wedge (separate into slices, if desired), and drizzle with dressing. Sprinkle evenly with shaved Parmesan cheese and salt and pepper to taste. Serve immediately.

Chicken BLT Salad

4 servings

prep: 15 minutes

½ cup garlic-and-herb-flavored cheese
  spread

3 cups chopped cooked chicken (about
  6 breasts)
½ cup grape tomatoes, halved
⅓ cup chopped scallion tops
2 bacon slices, cooked and crumbled
Salt and freshly ground black pepper to
  taste
Assorted mixed greens (optional)

1 Microwave cheese in a small microwave-safe bowl at HIGH 20 seconds.

2 Stir in chicken and next 3 ingredients,
tossing well. Add salt and pepper to
taste. Serve on assorted greens, if desired.

"I like to serve this chicken salad several
ways—with crackers, over lettuce leaves,
or in a sandwich.**"**

Taco Salad

6 servings

prep: 10 minutes   cook: 15 minutes

1½ pounds lean ground beef
1   (16-ounce) jar medium salsa
1   (16-ounce) can kidney beans,
        drained
2   tablespoons taco seasoning mix

2   avocados
½   cup sour cream
2   tablespoons chopped fresh cilantro

Bite-size tortilla chips
3   cups shredded lettuce (about ½ head)

1 Cook beef in a large nonstick skillet over medium-high heat, stirring until it crumbles and is no longer pink. Drain and return to skillet. Stir in salsa, beans, and taco seasoning; bring to a boil. Reduce heat, and simmer 10 minutes, stirring occasionally.

2 Peel and mash avocados; stir in sour cream and cilantro.

3 Place desired amount of tortilla chips on a serving platter, and top with shredded lettuce and beef mixture. Serve with avocado mixture and, if desired, chopped tomatoes, red onions, and shredded cheese.

Chopping Cilantro

Use kitchen shears to easily chop cilantro or any leafy herb in a measuring cup or small mixing bowl.

Sweet-and-Sour Slaw

12 servings

prep: 13 minutes   cook: 7 minutes

2   (3-ounce) packages Ramen noodles

¼   cup butter
½   cup sliced almonds

¼   cup olive oil
2   tablespoons sugar
2   tablespoons white vinegar
1½ teaspoons soy sauce
¼   teaspoon salt
1   large cabbage, finely shredded
      (about 8 cups)

1 Remove seasoning packets from noodle packages, and reserve for another use. Break up uncooked noodles.

2 Melt butter in a large skillet over medium-high heat; add noodle pieces and almonds. Cook, stirring constantly, 5 minutes or until toasted. Remove noodles and almonds from heat.

3 Whisk together olive oil and next 4 ingredients in a large bowl. Add cabbage, tossing to coat. Sprinkle with toasted noodles and almonds before serving.

❝ *Toss together this crowd-pleasing slaw the next time you need to take a dish to a potluck—it's a guaranteed winner!* **❞**

Dashing Desserts

"Whether you're seeking a grand finale to your special meal or just a little treat, you'll be able to satisfy your sweet tooth with any one of these tempting choices!"

Vanilla Spice Roasted Fruit

6 servings

prep: 3 minutes   cook: 25 minutes

¼	cup sugar
½	teaspoon ground cinnamon
4	cups frozen sliced peaches, unthawed
2	cups frozen pitted dark sweet cherries, unthawed
1	teaspoon vanilla extract

1 Preheat the oven to 450°. Stir together sugar and cinnamon in a small bowl. Cover a rimmed baking sheet with foil, and generously butter. Place fruit on baking sheet, and sprinkle with sugar mixture. Toss well then spread in a single layer.

2 Bake at 450° for 25 minutes or until juices are syrupy and fruit is tender. Remove from oven; place fruit in a medium bowl, and stir in vanilla. Serve warm over vanilla ice cream or cake slices.

"Serving this tasty dessert is a good way to get fruit into your diet. The fruit tenderizes as it roasts in the oven, and a thick syrup forms as the sugar melts—yum-my!**"**

Chocolate-Dipped Cookies

about 2 dozen

prep: 15 minutes

4 (1-ounce) semisweet chocolate
  baking squares
2 tablespoons butter
½ tablespoon shortening

3 (5.3-ounce) boxes shortbread
  cookies
Toppings: finely chopped toasted pecans,
  crushed hard peppermint candies,
  toasted sweetened flaked coconut,
  red or green candy sprinkles

1 Microwave chocolate, butter, and shortening in a small microwave-safe bowl at HIGH 1 minute, stirring at 15-second intervals. Stir until smooth. (Higher wattage microwaves may cook in less time.)

2 Dip ends of cookies in melted chocolate, and roll in desired toppings. Place on a wax paper-lined cookie sheet, and let stand 30 minutes or until firm.

"You'll find shortbread cookies available in many different shapes. Use your favorite shortbread cookie or a variety for this recipe."

PB & Chocolate Pan Cookies

(pictured on page 175)

about 2 dozen

prep: 10 minutes   cook: 20 minutes

¾   cup chunky peanut butter
2   large eggs
1   teaspoon vanilla extract

1   cup packed light brown sugar
2   cups biscuit baking mix
1   (12-ounce) package dark chocolate
      chips, divided

1 Preheat the oven to 325°. Stir together peanut butter, eggs, and vanilla in a large bowl.

2 Stir brown sugar into peanut butter mixture until combined. Add baking mix and ¾ cup dark chocolate chips, stirring just until moistened. Spread mixture on a lightly greased 10" x 15" rimmed baking sheet.

3 Bake at 325° for 20 minutes or until golden. Remove from oven, and sprinkle evenly with remaining 1¼ cups dark chocolate chips; let stand 5 minutes or until chocolate melts. Spread or drizzle melted chocolate over top of cookies. Cut into triangles, bars, or squares.

"Leave the electric beater in the cabinet—
you can mix this dough with a spoon for
a treat that combines everybody's favorite
flavors—chocolate and peanut butter! **"**

Butterscotch Drops

about 2½ dozen

prep: 15 minutes

1   (6-ounce) package butterscotch chips
     (see tip)

1   cup dry-roasted peanuts
1   cup shoestring potato sticks, broken
     into pieces

1 Melt chips in a saucepan over low heat.

2 Stir in peanuts and potato sticks. Drop by teaspoonfuls onto wax paper, and cool completely.

"Not only does this recipe have just 3 ingredients, but it's done in 15 minutes flat—from start to finish— and it's kid approved! Peanut butter chips offer up a good alternative to the butterscotch chips if you'd like a substitute.**"**

Hello Dolly Cookie Tarts

1 dozen

prep: 12 minutes   cook: 15 minutes

Nonstick cooking spray

½   (16.5-ounce) package refrigerated
      sugar cookie dough
1   cup sweetened flaked coconut
¾   cup semisweet chocolate chips
¾   cup chopped pecans
1   cup sweetened condensed milk

1 Preheat the oven to 350°. Place foil baking cups in a lightly greased muffin pan, and coat baking cups with nonstick cooking spray.

2 Cut cookie dough into 12 (¼") slices then press onto the bottom and two-thirds up sides of liners with floured fingers. Sprinkle each cup evenly with coconut, chocolate chips, and pecans; pour condensed milk over top.

3 Bake at 350° for 15 minutes or until tarts are lightly browned. Serve warm or at room temperature.

❝*These gooey tarts can easily stick to your muffin pan. Be sure to spray the pan first and then spray each foil baking cup for an easy breezy cleanup!*❞

Lemon-Blackberry Cream Puffs

6 servings

prep: 10 minutes   cook: 20 minutes

1   (10-ounce) package frozen puff
      pastry shells

2   cups fresh blackberries, divided

1   cup whipping cream
1   tablespoon confectioners' sugar
3   tablespoons lemon curd

1 Preheat the oven to 400°. Arrange shells on an ungreased baking sheet. Bake at 400° for 20 minutes or until lightly browned. Let cool slightly. Cut around center of pastry, and remove soft dough inside. Let cool completely.

2 Meanwhile, coarsely mash half the blackberries.

3 Beat whipping cream and sugar in a medium bowl at high speed of an electric beater until stiff peaks form (see tip on page 191). Whisk in lemon curd; fold in mashed blackberries.

4 To serve, arrange pastry shells on individual serving plates; spoon mixture evenly into shells. Sprinkle with remaining whole blackberries.

❝*All it takes is 5 ingredients to whip up this simple, refreshing dessert!*❞

Strawberries- & Chocolate Mousse-Topped Brownies

6 servings

prep: 7 minutes

1 (16-ounce) container fresh strawberries
2 tablespoons balsamic vinegar
1 tablespoon sugar

1 cup whipping cream
⅓ cup confectioners' sugar
2 tablespoons unsweetened cocoa

6 (1½" x 3½") unfrosted brownies

1 Remove and discard stems from strawberries. Cut strawberries in half, and place in a medium bowl. Sprinkle strawberries with vinegar and sugar; toss well, and set aside.

2 Beat whipping cream, confectioners' sugar, and cocoa in a medium bowl at low speed of an electric beater until soft peaks form (see tip on page 191).

3 Place brownies on individual serving plates. Top brownies evenly with strawberries and chocolate mousse. Serve immediately.

"*Store-bought brownies are elevated to new heights when topped with strawberries and homemade chocolate mousse. And it's sooo easy to do!***"**

Toasted Angel Food Cake with Honey Cream

4 servings

prep: 9 minutes   cook: 15 minutes

4   (2"-thick) slices angel food cake
2   tablespoons butter, melted

¾   cup whipping cream
¼   cup honey
¼   cup sour cream

Fresh blueberries

1 Preheat the oven to 350°. Arrange slices of angel food cake on a baking sheet, and brush tops with melted butter. Bake at 350° for 15 minutes or until light golden.

2 Beat whipping cream in a small bowl at medium-high speed of an electric beater until foamy (see tip); add honey and sour cream, beating until stiff peaks form.

3 To serve, top warm cake slices with honey cream and berries.

Whip It Up!

When beating whipping cream, make sure you start out with cold cream. Before you begin, place your mixing bowl and the beaters in the freezer for about 15 minutes. The colder the cream, the less likely it is to be overbeaten, to separate, and to turn to butter.

Banana Shortcakes with Candied Nuts

6 servings

prep: 7 minutes   cook: 23 minutes

6	large frozen biscuits
2	tablespoons melted butter
¼	cup sugar, divided
2	small bananas
1	tablespoon lemon juice
¾	cup whipping cream
½	cup chopped Southern praline-style pecans (see tip)

1 Brush frozen biscuit tops with melted butter; sprinkle each with 1 teaspoon sugar. Bake biscuits according to package directions.

2 Meanwhile, slice bananas, and toss with lemon juice. Place half the banana slices in a small bowl, and mash until smooth; reserve remaining banana slices.

3 Beat whipping cream and remaining sugar in a medium bowl at high speed of an electric beater until stiff peaks form (see tip on page 191). Fold in mashed banana and reserved banana slices.

4 To serve, split warm biscuits, and spoon banana cream evenly on bottom halves. Sprinkle with chopped praline-style pecans, and replace tops.

❝We used praline-style pecans as a topping for these shortcakes, but feel free to substitute other candied nuts or toffee bits as you desire.**❞**

Double Cherry Turnovers

9 turnovers

prep: 16 minutes   cook: 14 minutes

½ (17.3-ounce) package frozen puff
   pastry sheets, thawed
9 teaspoons cherry preserves
¾ cup frozen cherries

1 large egg white
1 tablespoon water
1 tablespoon turbinado sugar

1 Preheat the oven to 425°. Roll puff pastry into a 12" x 12" square; cut into 9 (4") squares. Spoon 1 teaspoon cherry preserves on each square; top evenly with frozen cherries.

2 Whisk together egg white and water. Brush edges of each square with egg white mixture. Fold each square into a triangle, pressing edges to seal. Brush top of each pastry with remaining egg white mixture, and sprinkle evenly with sugar. Place turnovers on a parchment paper-lined baking sheet. Bake at 425° for 12 to 14 minutes.

" *Every now and then, I like a little something sweet in the morning, and these turnovers are just the ticket! They're just oozing with tasty cherry filling—and just as great served for dessert, too!* **"**

Quick Tiramisù

6 to 8 servings

prep: 14 minutes

1	cup warm water
2	tablespoons sugar
1	tablespoon powdered espresso
4	ounces mascarpone cheese
2	(14-ounce) packages individual vanilla pudding packs
¾	cup frozen whipped topping, thawed
2	(3-ounce) packages cake-style ladyfingers (see tip)
1	teaspoon unsweetened cocoa

1 Combine first 3 ingredients, stirring until sugar dissolves.

2 Beat mascarpone and pudding together in a medium bowl at medium speed of an electric beater until smooth; fold in whipped topping.

3 Split ladyfingers in half lengthwise. Arrange 16 halves in a single layer in an 8" square baking dish. Drizzle with ⅓ cup coffee mixture. Spread one-third of pudding mixture evenly over ladyfingers. Repeat procedure twice with remaining ladyfingers, coffee mixture, and pudding mixture; sprinkle with cocoa. Serve immediately, or cover and chill until ready to serve.

The Tip on Ladyfingers

Cake-style ladyfingers can be found in the produce section of most supermarkets, usually next to the strawberries. Don't confuse these with the hard ladyfinger cookies that are found in the cookie section—you wouldn't have quite the same results if you used the hard variety instead!

Rocky Road Sundae Cake

4 servings

prep: 6 minutes   cook: 4 minutes

¼ cup whipping cream
1 cup semisweet chocolate chips

4 (1"-thick) slices pound cake, toasted
1 cup miniature marshmallows
½ cup chopped pecans
2 cups vanilla ice cream

1 Preheat the broiler. Heat whipping cream in a saucepan over medium heat 1 minute or until warm. Add chocolate chips; cook, stirring constantly, 1 minute until chocolate melts. Remove from heat.

2 Pour 2 tablespoons chocolate sauce over each slice of pound cake. Top evenly with marshmallows and pecans. Broil 1 to 2 minutes or until marshmallows are toasted (see tip). Top each pound cake slice with ice cream, and spoon remaining chocolate sauce over ice cream.

"The toasted marshmallows taste like you just heated them over a campfire. Watch them carefully, though, when broiling 'cause they'll burn quickly."

Apple Crêpes with Caramel Topping

3 servings

prep: 2 minutes   cook: 5 minutes

1   (12-ounce) package frozen apples

2   teaspoons brown sugar
¼   teaspoon apple pie spice
3   ready-to-use crêpes

Vanilla ice cream
Caramel topping

1 Prepare apples according to package directions.

2 Sprinkle brown sugar and apple pie spice over apples; stir well. Spoon ⅓ cup apple mixture onto center of each crêpe. Roll up crêpes. Place crêpes on a microwave-safe plate. Microwave at HIGH 10 seconds or until heated.

3 Top each crêpe with ice cream and caramel topping. Serve immediately.

"Keep these ingredients on hand so you can always have a simple dessert ready in a flash.**"**

Carrot Cake-Cheesecake Parfaits

4 servings

prep: 20 minutes

4 ounces cream cheese
¼ cup sugar, divided
⅔ cup whipping cream

½ teaspoon ground cinnamon
1 (8-ounce) can crushed pineapple, drained
⅓ cup grated carrot (about 1 carrot)
⅓ cup finely chopped pecans, toasted
⅓ cup flaked coconut

1 Place cream cheese and 2 tablespoons sugar in a small mixing bowl. Beat at low speed of an electric beater 1 to 2 minutes or until fluffy. Add whipping cream (see tip on page 191), and beat until stiff peaks form.

2 Mix remaining 2 tablespoons sugar and the cinnamon in a small bowl. Add pineapple and remaining ingredients; toss well.

3 Spoon half the cream cheese mixture into 4 (8-ounce) stemmed glasses or dessert dishes; top with half the pineapple mixture. Repeat layers. Serve immediately, or refrigerate until ready to serve.

Classy Containers

Be creative when selecting containers for such desserts as parfaits, mousses, soufflés, and gelatins. Wine goblets and champagne flutes are easy and attractive options.

Banana-Berry Split

(pictured on page 4)

2 to 4 servings

prep: 5 minutes

2   bananas, sliced in half lengthwise
6   scoops vanilla ice cream

½   cup hot fudge sauce
1   cup fresh blackberries
1   cup fresh raspberries
½   cup chopped peanuts

1 Place 2 banana halves in a dessert dish; add 3 scoops vanilla ice cream between banana halves.

2 Top with half each of hot fudge sauce, blackberries, raspberries, and chopped peanuts. Repeat procedure with remaining ingredients in another dessert dish.

"*This dessert fixes up fast—in just 5 minutes! Let your appetite dictate how much this treat serves—2 if you and a friend are ravenous or 4 if you're in the mood for sharing with the gang. Either way, this banana split is berry good!***"**

Chocolate-Coconut-Cookie Parfaits

6 servings

prep: 18 minutes

1⅓ cups heavy whipping cream
⅓   cup sour cream
2   tablespoons confectioners' sugar
1⅓ cups coarsely crushed dark
     chocolate-filled butter sandwich
     cookies (about 11 cookies) (such as
     Milano cookies)
6   tablespoons flaked coconut, toasted
     and divided

½   cup chocolate fudge sauce

1 Beat whipping cream, sour cream, and confectioners' sugar in a large mixing bowl at high speed of an electric beater until stiff peaks form (see tip on page 191). Fold in crushed cookies and 3 tablespoons coconut.

2 Layer half the cream mixture in stemmed glasses; top with 1 tablespoon fudge sauce. Repeat layers; sprinkle evenly with remaining coconut.

❝*These parfaits are fancy-sounding and fancy-looking, but they are ooh-so-easy to make. It takes less than 20 minutes to put together this elegant dessert!* **❞**

Poached Peach Sundaes

4 servings

prep: 5 minutes   cook: 18 minutes

½   cup honey
3   tablespoons butter
4   large peaches, peeled, halved, and
        pitted

2   cups vanilla ice cream
Toffee bits

1 Combine honey and butter in a medium saucepan; bring to a light boil over medium heat. Add peach halves, turning to coat; reduce heat to low, and simmer 15 minutes or until tender, stirring occasionally.

2 Transfer peaches to serving dishes; place a scoop of ice cream on top of peaches. Drizzle with syrup, and sprinkle with toffee bits.

It's Peachy Good!

This "naked" cobbler is perfect for celebrating one of our favorite summer fruits. Choose very ripe peaches to make an extra-juicy syrup. To speed up the ripening process, place peaches in a loosely closed paper bag at room temperature for 1 to 3 days. Check the peaches daily because ripening can occur very rapidly. They're ripe when the peaches yield slightly to gentle pressure.

Chocolate-Raspberry Mousse Parfaits

4 servings

prep: 15 minutes

⅔ cup whipping cream
¼ cup plus 2 tablespoons dark
    chocolate sauce

8 chocolate wafer cookies
8 teaspoons seedless raspberry jam
½ cup fresh raspberries

1 Beat cream in a small mixing bowl at high speed of an electric beater until stiff peaks form (see tip on page 191). Fold in chocolate sauce.

2 Crumble 1 wafer in bottom of each of 4 parfait glasses; dollop each wafer with 1 teaspoon jam. Spoon one-half of mousse in glasses, dividing evenly. Top with one-half of raspberries.

3 Repeat layers once. Serve immediately, or chill up to 8 hours.

❝*Don't let the name scare you; these parfaits are fancy enough for company but easy enough to make on a weeknight.*❞

Tropical Mango Shake

4 cups

prep: 12 minutes

2   cups cubed refrigerated mango slices
1   pint mango sorbet
¼   cup coconut milk
1   cup vanilla ice cream

½   cup sweetened flaked coconut,
      toasted (optional)

1 Process first 3 ingredients in an electric blender until smooth, stopping to scrape down sides. Add ice cream; process until smooth, stopping to scrape down sides as needed.

2 Pour shake into stemmed glasses; sprinkle with coconut, if desired. Serve immediately.

"*Using jarred, sliced mangoes helps make preparing this decadent dessert quick and easy. Enjoy this thick shake with a spoon if you opt for a topping of flaked coconut.***"**

Spiced Honey Sauce

1¼ cups

prep: 5 minutes   cook: 8 minutes

1   cup honey
6   tablespoons whipping cream
1   (3") cinnamon stick
1   teaspoon ground ginger

1   tablespoon unsalted butter
1   teaspoon vanilla extract
Dash of salt

1 Combine first 4 ingredients in a 2½-quart saucepan (see tip); bring to a boil over medium-high heat, stirring frequently. Cook about 5 more minutes, stirring occasionally.

2 Remove mixture from heat. Remove and discard cinnamon stick. Whisk butter, vanilla, and salt into mixture. Serve warm or cold over ice cream, waffles, fruit, pound cake, or cheesecake slices. Store in a jar in the refrigerator.

Saucepan Savvy

Don't be tempted to use a smaller saucepan for this recipe. The mixture foams to more than twice the volume when it first comes to a boil. So use the recommended 2½-quart saucepan.

METRIC EQUIVALENTS

The recipes that appear in this cookbook use the standard U.S. method for measuring liquid and dry or solid ingredients (teaspoons, tablespoons, and cups). The information in the following charts is provided to help cooks outside the United States successfully use these recipes. All equivalents are approximate.

EQUIVALENTS FOR DIFFERENT TYPES OF INGREDIENTS

A standard cup measure of a dry or solid ingredient will vary in weight depending on the type of ingredient. A standard cup of liquid is the same volume for any type of liquid. Use the following chart when converting standard cup measures to grams (weight) or milliliters (volume).

Standard Cup	Fine Powder (ex. flour)	Grain (ex. rice)	Granular (ex. sugar)	Liquid Solids (ex. butter)	Liquid (ex. milk)
1	140 g	150 g	190 g	200 g	240 ml
¾	105 g	113 g	143 g	150 g	180 ml
⅔	93 g	100 g	125 g	133 g	160 ml
½	70 g	75 g	95 g	100 g	120 ml
⅓	47 g	50 g	63 g	67 g	80 ml
¼	35 g	38 g	48 g	50 g	60 ml
⅛	18 g	19 g	24 g	25 g	30 ml

DRY INGREDIENTS BY WEIGHT

(To convert ounces to grams, multiply the number of ounces by 30.)

1 oz	=	¹⁄₁₆ lb	=	30 g
4 oz	=	¼ lb	=	120 g
8 oz	=	½ lb	=	240 g
12 oz	=	¾ lb	=	360 g
16 oz	=	1 lb	=	480 g

LENGTH

(To convert inches to centimeters, multiply the number of inches by 2.5.)

1 in			=	2.5 cm		
6 in	=	½ ft	=	15 cm		
12 in	=	1 ft	=	30 cm		
36 in	=	3 ft	=	1 yd	=	90 cm
40 in			=	100 cm	=	1 meter

LIQUID INGREDIENTS BY VOLUME

¼ tsp					=	1 ml		
½ tsp					=	2 ml		
1 tsp					=	5 ml		
3 tsp	=	1 tbls			=	½ fl oz	=	15 ml
		2 tbls	=	⅛ cup	=	1 fl oz	=	30 ml
		4 tbls	=	¼ cup	=	2 fl oz	=	60 ml
		5⅓ tbls	=	⅓ cup	=	3 fl oz	=	80 ml
		8 tbls	=	½ cup	=	4 fl oz	=	120 ml
		10⅔ tbls	=	⅔ cup	=	5 fl oz	=	160 ml
		12 tbls	=	¾ cup	=	6 fl oz	=	180 ml
		16 tbls	=	1 cup	=	8 fl oz	=	240 ml
		1 pt	=	2 cups	=	16 fl oz	=	480 ml
		1 qt	=	4 cups	=	32 fl oz	=	960 ml
						33 fl oz	=	1000 ml = 1 liter

COOKING/OVEN TEMPERATURES

	Fahrenheit	Celsius	Gas Mark
Freeze Water	32° F	0° C	
Room Temperature	68° F	20° C	
Boil Water	212° F	100° C	
Bake	325° F	160° C	3
	350° F	180° C	4
	375° F	190° C	5
	400° F	200° C	6
	425° F	220° C	7
	450° F	230° C	8
Broil			Grill

Index

FAVORITE RECIPES

Jot down the family's and your favorite recipes for handy-dandy fast reference.
And don't forget to include the dishes that drew "oohs" and "aahs" when you had the gang over.

Recipe	Source/Page	Remarks